Two Legends

ANDRÉ GIDE

Two Legends

Oedipus

AND

Theseus

TRANSLATED FROM THE FRENCH BY
John Russell

VINTAGE BOOKS

A DIVISION OF RANDOM HOUSE

New York

A Note on Œdipus and Theseus

by John Russell

André Gide was always fascinated by the history and mythology of the ancient world, which furnished him throughout his career with a vast repertory of symbolic events—the prototypes, in short, of many of those which have most affected us in the last fifty years. Herodotus and the Bible served him, at the turn of the century, in the creation of Saul and Le Roi Candaule; Prometheus is not only the hero of one of his most original works, but an ever present image of hardihood; and even his reflections on the Soviet Union are prefaced with a long allusion to Demeter. The two works in this present volume, though superficially incongruous (the one is a play, dating from 1930, and the other a philosophical *nouvelle*, written a dozen years later), are linked by a common preoccupation with the myth of Œdipus and the possibility of its reinterpretation in modern terms.

Œdipus is mercifully remote from those modern adaptations in which the text lumbers, for good or ill, in the tracks of Sophocles until eventually the admired actor of the day can be led, bleeding and ululant, from the stage. In Gide's play human dignity puts the horrors in their place; and for the spectator its appeal is rather to the intelligence than to any variety of primitive astonishment. It is basically a stringent intellectual debate; as in the masterpieces of

Poussin (a painter whom Gide particularly admired) the realities of physical violence are subordinated to the grand, overmastering instincts of order and design. The Œdipus whom Gide evokes is not the Œdipus of Freudian legend. To this Œdipus the disasters of his family history are merely incidental to a greater misfortune—the failure, as it seems, of his ambition to make Man independent of the gods. It is this theme that recurs in *Theseus*; and it was at André Gide's suggestion that the two compositions were brought together.

Theseus was the last of Gide's works, but it was one that had been long projected. For more than thirty years the idea had possessed him, from time to time, of committing to paper a new manipulation of this ancient legend. Other images of Theseus reverberate, as is natural, within this new version. The Theseus of Plutarch is here, even down to the feathery branches of asparagus among which the beardless hero carried out the first of his summary but appreciative sexual experiments. The Theseus of Racine is here, forever aghast at the murderous favors accorded to him by the gods. But Gide's Theseus is a different, more constructive character. He discourses to us in the cloudless evening of his life, with the motiveless lechery of his early manhood quite laid aside, and the more disreputable episodes (so carefully husbanded by Plutarch) discounted as fables. Nor do we see him reduced, like the Theseus of Racine, to the point at which an anonymous exile alone offers the possibility of requital. It is rather for Œdipus to propose this point of view, in the dialogue that closes the book. This Theseus eventually surmounts his private griefs, and sets himself to found a great city, governed by an

aristocracy of the intellect. It is as an old and lonely
man that we leave him, but one secure in his glory;
and these last pages resume the dialogue between
Christian and non-Christian laws that has always
been, for Gide, at once brake and accelerator.

One can distinguish many others among the elements that Gide metamorphosed for our enjoyment.
The full-scale evocation of ancient Crete owes something to Flaubert, something to Sir Arthur Evans; but
the essentials of tone and pace, the golden sensuality
and the pondered detail, are Gide's alone. And what
concept could be more Gidian than that of the ordeal
in the labyrinth—an ordeal, not of endurance, but of
pleasure? In the Minotaur himself, that flower-struck
beauty, lulled into hebetude by the delights of his
surroundings, we glimpse the Sudanese Negroes
whom Gide had watched in Tunis, more than sixty
years ago, stuffing flowers into their nostrils.

Present and past are mingled, moreover, in the con-
struction of Theseus himself. Pre-Roman and post-
Renaissance traits have coalesced in this egregious
hero. Wraith-like, other admirations of Gide's—not
to speak of Gide himself—compose part of Theseus;
nor can all these affinities be passed on to the English
reader, since some of them may be descried only
through verbal parallels in the original text. When
Theseus says: *"Je n'ai jamais aimé la demeure, fût-ce
au sein des délices,"* it is possible to recall that Gide
has written of his old friend Paul Valéry that *"Fût-ce
dans les delices, il ne lui plaisait pas d'attarder."*

Valéry had always symbolized, for Gide, an ideal,
undistractible vigor; and Theseus, too, is endowed
with the same grand individualism. Theseus at times
is not so much man as a committee, with Gide at its

head. When Theseus forswears private enjoyments and dedicates himself to the salvation of Athens, he remarks: *"il ne s'agissait plus de conquérir, mais de regner."* One cannot but remember the lines from *Bérénice* which Gide quoted in 1941 in order to show that Racine did sometimes allow higher interests to overrule the claims of love. Theseus here echoes Titus:

Je sens bien que sans vous je ne saurais plus vivre.
Mais il ne s'agit plus de vivre, il faut regner.

Olympian Goethe takes his place on the committee, beside Valéry and beside Racine's Titus. For whereas, in politics, Theseus pursues a modified Stalinism, and he has, in the life of the senses, the uninhibited command of enjoyment which Gide tried to transplant from the Tunis of 1894 in the western Europe of our own epoch, he also derives, in religion and in personal morality, from the Goethe whom Gide pictured in his preface to the Pléiade edition of Goethe's plays. Even his motto, *"Passez outre,"* which clangs like a bell-buoy throughout the story, is attributed also to Goethe. Theseus, as much as Goethe, valued love as a liberating force; and, like him, he knew when to have done with it. Nor can one fail to detect the Goethean affirmations that Theseus opposes to the mysticism of the transfigured Œdipus. There Theseus makes, on Gide's behalf, an act of confidence. The story of Theseus, once begun, took on a panoramic aspect, as if Gide were out to display every resource of art and language, and to rediscover his own spiritual history in the story of the founder of Athens. No palpable city bears witness to Gide's own long effort; but he passed on his conviction that man has not yet said his last word; in his last years he gathered up the ends of a lifetime of work; his language took on a definitive grandeur; and it became only just to acclaim him, as he acclaimed Goethe, as "the finest example, at once grave and smiling, of what man can wrest from himself without the help of Grace."

I should like to express my gratitude to Madame Simon Bussy, who, with signal generosity, has allowed me to profit by her unique experience and authority as translator of Gide.

CONTENTS

A NOTE ON ŒDIPUS AND THESEUS

V

ŒDIPUS

3

THESEUS

47

Oedipus

to BERNARD GROETHUYSEN

CHARACTERS:

ŒDIPUS

TIRESIAS

JOCASTA

CREON

ANTIGONE

ETEOCLES

POLYNICES

ISMENE

CHORUS

ACT I

ŒDIPUS: Here I am, all present and complete in this
instant of everlasting time; like someone who
might come down to the front of the stage and
say:

I am Œdipus. Forty years old, and for twenty
years a king. With my own strong arm I have
pulled myself up to the highest point of happiness. A waif and a foundling, without papers or
citizenship, I am glad above all that I owe nothing to anyone but myself. Happiness was not
given to me; I conquered it. That way compla-
cency lurks; and to guard against it I wondered
at first if my case was not one of predestination.
Fearful of that giddying pride which has un-
steadied certain leaders—and they not the least
famous— But there you are, Œdipus, off again on
those overlong phrases that you don't always
know how to finish. Just say simply what you have
to say, and don't go in for that inflated manner

which you claim to have cut out of your life.
Keep things simple and they'll turn out all right.
Be simple yourself: direct as an arrow—straight
to the target. . . . That brings me back to what
I was saying just now: Yes, if I sometimes manage
to think that I have been launched on my way by
the gods, I do it to redouble my own modesty
and to refer back to them the credit for my
destiny. For in my particular case it's rather
difficult not to get a little puffed-up about oneself. I escape it by creating above me a holy
power to which, whether I like it or not, I am
subject. Who would not gladly bow down to such
a power, if it led him to where I now am? A god
is guiding you, Œdipus, and there aren't two like
you. That's what I tell myself on Sundays and
holidays. The rest of the week I've no time to
think about it. Besides, what would be the use?
I'm no good at reasoning; logic's not my strong
point; I proceed by intuition. Some people, whenever they get mixed up in the traffic, keep saying
to themselves: "Should I give way? Have I the
right to overtake?" For my part, I always behave
as if a god were telling me what to do.

⟨*The Chorus, divided into two groups, comes
downstage, to right and left of Œdipus.*⟩

BOTH CHORUSES: We, the Chorus, whose particular
function in this place is to represent the opinion
of the majority, declare ourselves surprised and
grieved by the profession of so aggressive an
individualism. The views that Œdipus has dis-
closed are intolerable in other people—unless
they are disguised.

Of course it is a good thing to put the gods on one's side. But the surest way is to be on the side of the priests. Œdipus would do well to consult Tiresias; he's the man who's really got the gods in hand. Under pretense of serving our interest, Œdipus runs the risk of turning them against us, and there's no doubt that it is to him that we owe the evils which are overwhelming us at this moment. (*In a lower voice*) We shall try, with inexpensive sacrifices and well-directed prayers, to earn their indulgence; and, by dissociating ourselves from our king, to direct against him alone the chastisement that his pride deserves.

RIGHT-HAND CHORUS (*to Œdipus*): That you yourself are happy, no one would deny, though you do say it too often. But we are not happy, we, your people, O Œdipus; but we, your people—ah, no, we are not happy. We should prefer to hide it from you; but the action of this drama could not proceed unless we give you a most lamentable piece of news. The plague—since we must give it its real name—continues to bring mourning to Thebes. Your family has so far been spared; but it is seemly that a king should interest himself in his people's misfortunes, even where these do not affect him directly.

LEFT-HAND CHORUS: Besides, we can't help thinking that your happiness and our unhappiness are linked in some mystical way; at least, that is what Tiresias' teaching has allowed us to glimpse. It is good that we should get this point quite straight. Apollo must give us the facts. You yourself have been good enough to dispatch the excellent

Creon, your brother-in-law, to the sanctuary, and he will soon be here to give us the oracle's much-awaited answer.

OEDIPUS: Here he is, just back at this very moment. (*Enter Creon. To Creon*)

Well?

CREON: Wouldn't it be better if I spoke to you alone?

OEDIPUS: Why? You know I despise all forms of subterfuge. You shall therefore say everything in front of everyone. I invite, I command you to do so. If anything can remedy the evils of my people, they as much as I have the right to know it. Only thus can they help me to put things right. What did the oracle say?

CREON: Just what I expected: something is rotten in the kingdom.

OEDIPUS: Stop. The people are not enough. Your sister Jocasta and our four children must also be present.

CREON: One moment. I approve of your summoning Jocasta. You know that I am a man of the liveliest family feeling. Besides, she may give us valuable advice. But the children seem to me very young to take part in the discussion.

OEDIPUS: Antigone is already no longer a child. Eteocles and Polynices are what I was at their age: reckless, quick to act, and anything but stupid. It is a good thing that they should know something of anxiety. As for Ismene, she won't understand.

(*Enter Jocasta and Œdipus' four children*)

OEDIPUS (*to Jocasta*): Your brother is just back from Pytho. I wanted you all to be here with me to hear the god's answer. Come on, Creon, tell us now: what did the oracle say?

CREON: That the wrath of God would never be turned away from Thebes until Laius, the late king, had been avenged.

ŒDIPUS: Avenged of what?

CREON: Surely you know that the man whose place you have taken in my sister Jocasta's bed, and on the throne of Thebes, died at the hand of an assassin?

ŒDIPUS: Yes, I know—but was the culprit not punished?

CREON: The police could never lay hands on him. In fact, we must even admit that they never looked very hard.

ŒDIPUS (*to Jocasta*): You never told me—

JOCASTA: Every time I wanted to tell you, my dear, you interrupted me. "No, don't talk of the past," you burst out, "I don't want to know anything about it. A golden age has begun. All things are made anew. . . ."

CREON: The word "justice" was turned on your lips to "amnesty."

ŒDIPUS: If I knew the swine who—

JOCASTA: Calm yourself, my dear. It's ancient history. Why go back to the past?

ŒDIPUS: I won't keep calm. I only wish I had known it sooner. Damnation, I'll not rest till I find the culprit. I'll hunt him down, no matter where he's hiding. He'll not escape me—that I swear. How long ago did all this happen?

JOCASTA: I had been six months a widow when you succeeded Laius. That was twenty years ago.

ŒDIPUS: Twenty years of happiness—

TIRESIAS: —which in the sight of God are as one day. (*Tiresias, blind, dressed as a friar, has come in unnoticed, accompanied by Antigone and Ismene.*)

ŒDIPUS: God, what a bore that man is! Forever meddling in other people's business. Who asked you to come?

JOCASTA (*to Œdipus*): My dear, you shouldn't speak so before the children. It isn't wise to diminish the authority of the man whom we have chosen to be their tutor, and who has to go with them everywhere. (*To Tiresias*) You were saying—?

TIRESIAS: I do not wish to vex the king.

ŒDIPUS: It is not what people say that vexes me, but what they think and don't say. Speak.

TIRESIAS: Alone, and man to man, Œdipus, we will speak of your happiness—of what you call happiness. But for the present we must discuss the unhappiness of the people. The people are suffering, Œdipus, and their king cannot but know it. Between the prosperity of the few and the indigence of the majority, God weaves a mysterious thread. The name of God, Œdipus, is often on your lips; I don't blame you for that—far from it —but for seeking to make God your assentor instead of your judge, and for feeling no awe in His presence.

ŒDIPUS: I have never been what is called a funk.

TIRESIAS: The more valiant a leader may be before men, the more pleasing is his submissiveness to God.

ŒDIPUS: Had I felt awe in the presence of the Sphinx,

I could not have answered its riddle and I should not have been king.

BOTH CHORUSES: It's no good, Œdipus, it's no good. You know very well that with Tiresias even a king can't have the last word.

RIGHT-HAND CHORUS: No doubt you vanquished the Sphinx; but remember that afterwards you presumed, having solved the riddle, to do without the auguries of the birds.

LEFT-HAND CHORUS: And then when the birds troubled your sleep, you deceitfully told us that we could kill them off, in defiance of Tiresias.

BOTH CHORUSES: They made an excellent stew; but we realized that we had done wrong when God destroyed our crops with a plague of caterpillars.

RIGHT-HAND CHORUS: And if we fasted that year, it was from penitence, of course—

LEFT-HAND CHORUS: But also because we had nothing left to eat.

BOTH CHORUSES: And so from now on, in total obedience, we urge you to listen to Tiresias.

ŒDIPUS (*to his sons*): The people would always rather have a religious interpretation than explain things naturally—there's nothing to be done about it. (*To Tiresias*) All right—get on with it.

TIRESIAS: The royal police can seek out the criminal. But while we are waiting for them to find him, I beseech every one of you to show yourselves repentant; for every one of you is guilty before God. We cannot imagine a man without stain. Therefore let each of you descend into the depths of his being and there examine himself and repent. Meanwhile a few offerings may help to appease

Him whose displeasure has laid so severe a
scourge upon the town. The dead are already
beyond counting. I was walking just now with
Polynices and he, who saw what I cannot see,
will tell you—

POLYNICES: Yes, father, not far from the palace we
came upon a group of people smitten with the
plague. They were all smeared with vomit and
feces, and writhing in some terrible colic. It
seemed as if each were helping the other to die.
We could hear nothing, all around us, but their
weeping, and sighing, and hiccuping. And when
they looked at us—

CREON: Enough! Enough!

(*Ismene has fainted.*)

ŒDIPUS: Yes, quite enough! You've upset the little one
now!

ETEOCLES (*to Polynices*): You shouldn't have said
such things in front of your sister.

ŒDIPUS (*to Jocasta*): Be good enough to take the
children away. (*Tiresias leaves with them.*) Let
the people also leave us. I want to think.

(*Œdipus and Creon are left alone.*)

CREON: You are inconsequent, like all impulsive people. What was the point of that oath you swore
just now?

ŒDIPUS: What oath?

CREON: You see—you've forgotten it already. But the
people are there to remember it, and your children too. And Tiresias is there to bring it back to
your mind. You swore to avenge the king's death.

ŒDIPUS: That is true. Why was the criminal not
prosecuted?

CREON: The whole thing was hushed up.

ŒDIPUS: By whom?

CREON: By me at first. I was regent at the time, and I thought it imprudent to call the people's attention to it, and to let them see that a king may be killed like any other man.

ŒDIPUS: Yes, but they know it now.

CREON: Jocasta also opposed the idea of an inquiry. She thought—and very wisely—that nothing should be allowed to darken the first days of your reign.

ŒDIPUS: Jocasta has always watched over my happiness. She is perfect, Jocasta. What a wife! And what a mother! For me, who never knew my own mother, she has been wife and mother in one. Tell me—her first husband, did she really love him?

CREON: A great deal less than you, that's certain.

ŒDIPUS: And another thing—didn't they have any children?

CREON: That's a long story. I don't know if I should really tell you about it.

ŒDIPUS: Then you should not have begun. But now I insist on knowing.

CREON: Very well. They didn't want to have any children, because the oracle—

ŒDIPUS: That oracle again!

CREON: —had predicted that Laius would be stabbed to death by his own son. But, one festive evening, they were careless—

ŒDIPUS: I see what you mean. And what became of this child of drunkenness?

CREON: It was a son. As soon as he was born they gave

him over to a shepherd, whose sad duty it was to abandon him on the mountainside, where he was eaten by wild beasts.

ŒDIPUS: Is this shepherd still alive?

CREON: You ask too many questions. If you want my advice—don't fret about it. Live in peace.

ŒDIPUS: With such a thorn in my pillow, I fear I should never sleep soundly again. Besides, you heard what was said: it is God's will that the murderer should be punished.

CREON: My dear Œdipus, oracles are all very well for the people, but they can't dictate to us. We who rule should use them to reinforce our authority, and interpret them as suits us best. They told us that Laius would be killed by his son; but it was the son who died. Laius is dead, all the same, you may say. If he were alive, you would not be sitting on his throne. So don't distress yourself about his loss, and don't worry about the manner of his death. Whoever killed him did it for you; he played your game; it's not for you to punish him, but rather to give him a reward.

ŒDIPUS: And what would Tiresias say?

CREON: Are you afraid of him?

ŒDIPUS: Not exactly. But he has the ear of the people. And I myself sometimes find the sound of his voice disquieting—yes, the sound of it—it's as if it came from the nether world. Here he is again. He approaches, and yet one never hears his step. What do you want with us, Tiresias? (*Tiresias has come in.*)

TIRESIAS: Œdipus, the queen would like to speak to you. She is waiting for you in the palace.

(*Exit Œdipus. To Creon*)

Besides, I wanted him to leave us alone. I heard every word you were saying.

CREON: You were listening?

TIRESIAS: I can hear without listening. Even before I hear people's voices I know their thoughts. Creon, it is not a good thing that Œdipus should be reassured.

CREON: What do you mean?

TIRESIAS: His mind is already too much at rest. His soul is like some sealed vessel, to which fear can find no entrance. My authority is based on the fear of God, and there is blasphemy in Œdipus' untroubled happiness. It is for you, Creon, to start a little crack in that happiness.

CREON: Why?

TIRESIAS: Because it is by means of that disquieting little crack that God will find a way into his heart. Eteocles and Polynices are giving me the slip— with every day I feel more sure of it. Jocasta will confirm it: their father's example has persuaded them that they can cut free from the authority to which every man should bow. I do not speak to you in my own name, but in the name of the God whom I represent; in the name of Jocasta and of our pious Antigone; and in the name of the people, who live in terror, inferring from the scourge which now afflicts them that they are being punished for their king's incredulity. Moreover, how can Antigone revere a father, and Jocasta love a husband, whose heart has rejected the God whom both of them worship? You yourself, Creon, must see that it is in everyone's interest that a king should bow to a higher power to whom each and all may appeal—be it even against their king.

(*Enter Jocasta.*)

JOCASTA: Œdipus is dumbfounded by the news I have just given him: Antigone wishes to take orders.

CREON: Antigone a vestal!

TIRESIAS: It's not surprising. The dear child hopes in this way to offset her father's impiety.

JOCASTA: She has confided her intentions to me, but they are to remain a secret. Her brothers as yet know nothing of them.

CREON: Ah, poor child!

TIRESIAS: Why poor? She will find in God a surer happiness than any Œdipus can show—a saintly felicity consisting not in pride, but in humility.

CREON: I think too that she was much distressed by the misfortunes of the people.

JOCASTA: She begged me to let her nurse the sick. I protested that that could not be fit work for a princess. "Then let me pray for them, intercede for them," she said. And she added, more quietly: "and perhaps too for—" but could not go on for tears.

TIRESIAS: For someone yet more gravely ill.

CREON: Was she thinking of her father?

TIRESIAS: Of course. How did Œdipus take it?

JOCASTA: At first he was both angry and affronted. Then he cried out that he recognized Tiresias' hand in the matter.

TIRESIAS: I am merely God's instrument. But, since He is working through me, He will not now stay His hand.

JOCASTA: My beloved husband is all virtue, all constancy, all courage; that he should be brought to offer these things to God should be our dearest duty—that I know very well, Tiresias.

TIRESIAS: Creon must help me. He will break down the king's self-confidence and make him more disposed to accept what I say.

CREON: I shall be glad to try, but I can't promise to succeed. Œdipus does not readily listen to what bores him.

TIRESIAS: God will inspire you, as He has inspired me, with the way to touch him on the quick.

CREON: God has never inspired me very much.

TIRESIAS: Only to the blind does He give all His inspiration.

JOCASTA: I put myself in your hands, Tiresias, for it is through you that we learn the decisions of the Most High.

ACT II

(*Œdipus and Creon come downstage, in conversation.*)

CREON: If we were not so unlike each other, we should take less pleasure in our conversations. If I enjoy talking to you, dear brother-in-law, it is because you allow me to glimpse things that I should never have remarked for myself. Where you are all for novelty and experiment, I myself am bound by the past. Tradition I respect, and custom, and established law. But do you not agree that somebody in a state should stand for those things, and that I represent, vis-à-vis your spirit of initiative, a desirable counterpoise? I keep you from going too fast, I act as a brake on those over-venturesome projects of yours—they could often put the social system out of joint, you know, if I wasn't there to clog you and weigh you down. . . .

ŒDIPUS: (*absent-mindedly*): Perhaps.

CREON: Family feeling runs especially strong in me. You are one of my family, after all, and I am as

interested in your children as I am in my own.
Allow me to ask after Ismene's health. She is a
nervous child, and when she fainted yesterday,
while her brother was telling us—

ŒDIPUS: That's all over now.

CREON: All the same, you ought to see that she takes
more exercise. Jocasta too—I don't think she's
been very well for some little time. It upsets her
when things go badly for the people. You should
try to take her mind off it.

ŒDIPUS: Oh, quite. Quite.

CREON: And when we are less busy I must talk to you
about your two boys. Tiresias is a good teacher,
of course, but they don't seem to pay much attention to him. They're a couple of rebels—I can't
quite define it, but there's no doubt they get it
from you. Has Eteocles read you his reflections
on the malady of the age?

ŒDIPUS: On the plague?

CREON: No, no—the *Malady of the Age,* with the sub-
title: *Our Present Discontents.* Naturally his discontents are of a most elevated sort. He's a phe-
nomenon, that boy. And for good looks, strength,
and intelligence, Polynices is his equal. They
must both be like what you were at their age. I
expect you recognize yourself in them.

ŒDIPUS: Sometimes.

CREON: They are unquiet spirits. But at least they
have your example before their eyes. Whereas
you, feeling yourself a stranger at Polybius' court—
Is that why you went away? Weren't you at
ease in his palace?

ŒDIPUS: I? I lived like a fighting-cock. But, to begin
with, I don't enjoy being coddled. At that time I

believed I was Polybius' son. Then one day a
soothsayer came to the court and began telling
fortunes. Everybody wanted to consult him. My
turn came. He turned pale, refused to speak in
the hearing of the others, took me on one side,
and told me that I was destined to kill my father.
At first I laughed at his prediction, but he was so
sure of himself that I thought it best to take precautions; and the first of these was to speak
frankly to Polybius and to tell him that the surest
way not to fulfill this disastrous forecast was for
me to leave his court forever, much as it would
grieve me to do so, for I loved him. It was then,
and in order to reassure me, that he revealed to
me that I was not his child, that he had adopted
me, and that, as far as he was concerned, I therefore had nothing to fear. As to who had been my
father, he couldn't enlighten me. A shepherd,
while driving his flock to pasture, had found me
on the mountainside, hanging by one foot, like
a fruit, from the low branches of a shrub (that's
why I am slightly lame)—naked, exposed to wind
and rain, as if I had been the fruit of some clan-
destine passion, an unwanted, compromising
child. . . .

CREON: A bastard. Yes, I can understand that that
must be very painful.

ŒDIPUS: Oh, certainly not—I don't at all mind knowing that I am a bastard. When I thought I was
Polybius' son, I tried to ape his virtues. I kept
asking myself: "What is there in me that I do not
owe to my forefathers?" Attentive to the lesson of
the past, I looked only to yesterday for approval
and advice. Then suddenly the thread was broken.

I had gushed up from the unknown; no longer any past, no longer any father's example, nothing to lean on any more; everything to be built up anew—country, forefathers—all to be invented, all to be discovered. Nobody to take after but myself. What does it matter from that moment whether I am a Greek or a Welshman? O Creon, you who are so submissive, so orthodox in every way, how could you understand the splendor of such demands? To know nothing of one's parents is a summons to excel.

CREON: But all the same, why did you leave Polybius after he had given you this reassurance? He had adopted you, and had no children of his own. You had every hope of succeeding him on his throne.

ŒDIPUS: I detest that kind of promotion and want nothing that I have not earned on my own merits. Great qualities were dormant within me, and I could not bear them to lie quiescent. I felt that in the peace and comfort of Polybius' court I was missing my destiny.

CREON: It is quite natural that I should look at things differently. Had I been a bastard, perhaps I too should have striven to acquire such things, both spiritual and material, as had not come to me by lawful inheritance. But I was the son of one king and the brother of another. I cannot be other than conservative. Without being myself a king, I enjoyed at Laius' court, as I now enjoy at your own, all the advantages of a crown, with none of its burdens and anxieties.

ŒDIPUS: Enjoy them in peace, Creon, enjoy them in peace. No doubt it is all to the good that men of my temperament should be very rare. But I see the children coming. Let us listen to them without showing ourselves.

(*Œdipus and Creon withdraw to the side of the stage. Enter Antigone and Polynices.*)

POLYNICES: Free thought is impossible unless one first removes the twist that religious practices import to the mind.

ANTIGONE: If you give way to the passions, they too will warp the mind, and more dangerously. Yes, my mind has taken to itself the bent of only being able to think straight. I can promise you that there is no longer any impulse of my being but directs itself toward—

POLYNICES: Go on.

ANTIGONE: —directs itself toward God.

POLYNICES: Why didn't you say that at once?

ANTIGONE: Because I know that you don't believe in God.

POLYNICES: God is simply what you put at the far end of your thoughts. Do you really believe in Him?

ANTIGONE: With all my heart and with all my mind. If I were talking to anybody but you I should say: "with all my soul." But you don't believe in the soul either.

POLYNICES: Perhaps you'll end by making me believe in yours. But this God you speak of—does He exist apart from yourself?

ANTIGONE: Why yes, since it is He who draws me to Him.

POLYNICES: You simply see the reflection of your own virtues.

ANTIGONE: On the contrary, I am myself the reflection. There is no virtue but has its source in Him.

POLYNICES: Listen, Antigone. Don't blush at what I am going to ask you.

ANTIGONE: I am blushing already. But go on.

POLYNICES: Is one forbidden to marry one's sister?

ANTIGONE: Yes, of course—forbidden by God and man alike. Why do you ask?

POLYNICES: Because if I could marry you absolutely, I think I should let myself be guided by you toward your God.

ANTIGONE: How can one hope to attain what is good while doing what is evil?

POLYNICES: Good, evil—those are the only words you know.

ANTIGONE: Not a word comes to my lips that has not first been in my heart.

(*Creon and Œdipus are still in hiding, and remain so during the next scene.*)

CREON (*to Œdipus*): But look here! That's incest—I can't stomach that.

Œdipus: Be quiet.

(*Polynices and Antigone go off. Enter Eteocles and Ismene.*)

ISMENE: It's rare to find you alone—you're always with your brother. How do you manage to get on so well with him?

ETEOCLES: Surely it's natural that one's brother should understand one better than somebody from outside?

ISMENE: Antigone and I have such different tastes that I quarrel with her all the time. Whenever I like a thing, she reproaches me and says it's forbidden. I don't even dare to laugh or play in front of her. Of course she's older than I am, but really one would think she'd never been young.

ETEOCLES: Polynices and I were born and brought up together. We have everything in common. There isn't one of my pleasures, nor one of my thoughts, I believe, that is not also his—and is redoubled by being reflected in him.

ISMENE: I don't know that I should very much like to have a double. And if I had one, I should probably detest him. Besides, there are some things one can't share.

ETEOCLES: We haven't come across them yet.

ISMENE: All the same, if one of you fell in love—

ETEOCLES: Pooh! Perhaps we shall pick on twins.

ISMENE: And when it comes to being king?

ETEOCLES: We've already promised each other that we shall reign by turns.

ISMENE: And what if you don't find those twins? (*They laugh.*)

ETEOCLES: I must go and ask him about it. (*Exit Eteocles. Enter Antigone.*)

ANTIGONE: How can you laugh when the people are in mourning?

ISMENE: You don't laugh even when all goes well around you.

ANTIGONE: Everywhere on this earth there is, alas, more sorrow than joy.

ISMENE: Joy is within me, and I hear it singing in my heart. One doesn't make things any better by weeping for those who are unhappy. But you sympathize only with those who are in trouble. Other people's happiness puts you out of humor.

ANTIGONE: There are some people, Ismene, whose happiness is disquieting.

ISMENE: Some people?

ANTIGONE: My father's. The more I love him, the

more I fear the happiness of which he boasts. He leaves God out of account; and nothing can stand solidly that has not its base in God.

ISMENE: My joy is a wingèd thing.

(*They go off.*)

CREON: Well! They certainly put things well, those children of yours! "My joy is a wingèd thing"— I must remember that. As for Antigone, it may not have seemed very much, but it's very deep, you know, what she was saying. Just what I wanted to make you feel, but I didn't know quite how to go about it.

ŒDIPUS: What do you mean?

CREON: Why, that your happiness doesn't seem to me so well founded as all that. But now let's listen to your boys.

(*Enter Eteocles and Polynices.*)

ETEOCLES: Let's get down to it. What is that we look for in books? It's always, in greater or less degree, an authorization. Even those who claim to be in love with order and to respect things as they are, those whom Tiresias calls "right-thinking people"—what they want from books is authority to bore, oppress, and terrorize their neighbors. What they want is some maxim, some theory that will make their consciences comfortable and put them themselves on the side of the right.

POLYNICES: And what we, the wrong-thinkers, are after is authority to do what tradition and good form, or the law with its apparatus of fear and constraint, have told us not to do.

ETEOCLES: In other words, freedom to behave indecently.

POLYNICES: Yes, more or less—something like that.

ETEOCLES: For instance, I'm looking at this moment for a phrase that will authorize me to sleep with Ismene.

CREON (*to Œdipus*): Vicious little brute!

POLYNICES: With your sister?

ETEOCLES: With our sister. What of it?

POLYNICES: If you find it—pass it on to me.

CREON: Two vicious little brutes!

ŒDIPUS (*to Creon*): Get out.

(*Exit Creon.*)

ETEOCLES: If I find what?

POLYNICES: That authorization. But there's another remedy—more general, and therefore easier to find. I mean, you could do without authority altogether.

ETEOCLES: Oh, well, I haven't spent my time searching in books for that—

POLYNICES: You mean you've just acted upon it?

ETEOCLES: What do you think? If I'm now looking out for an honorable motive, it's rather for her sake—

POLYNICES: For Ismene's?

ETEOCLES: Yes, for Ismene's. Personally I don't care a damn.

POLYNICES: And if I were to break your jaw, personally—would you begin to care a little?

ETEOCLES: Try it and see. . . . You jealous! Haven't we shared everything up to now? Was I wrong to confide in you? And besides, you great idiot, it's not true. I only said it to provoke you.

POLYNICES: Will you swear there's nothing between you and Ismene?

ETEOCLES: Up to now, no. I'm holding back.

POLYNICES: Not as much as I am.

ETEOCLES: If I hadn't told you about it, the idea would never have entered your head.

POLYNICES: That's to say I shouldn't have known my own thoughts. There are lots of things we think of without knowing it.

ETEOCLES: That's what our dreams are made of.

POLYNICES: Don't you ever wonder what are the limits of human thought? In my last ode I compare thought to a dragon of which as a rule we know only the body and that part, the tail, which drags along in the past; a sphinx, one might say, whose invisible nostrils are somewhere inside me, scenting, snuffling, nosing about. Nothing is safe from its disruptive curiosity. The rest of its body follows as and when it can.

ETEOCLES: That is the dragon I call "the malady of the age." I too feel it within me, forever asking, asking. It's fairly eating me up with questions.

POLYNICES: I am thinking of the dragon that Cadmus slew. They say that from his teeth we sprang.

ETEOCLES: You believe in that, Polynices? They also say that Semele, who was Cadmus' daughter, and a mortal, carried Bacchus the god within her womb. In our present state of advanced civilization, and now that our father has killed the last of the sphinxes, gods and monsters no longer inhabit the upper air or the open countryside; they are within us.

POLYNICES: Cadmus, Lycus, and Amphion, to whom we owe the alphabet by which thought has been preserved. . . . Ah, how old humanity seems to me, and how distant all of that! I dream of the age when speech itself had not yet been invented.

ETEOCLES: Tiresias tells us that speech came to men as a gift from the gods.

POLYNICES: I would rather believe in heroes than in gods.

(*Œdipus approaches his sons.*)

ŒDIPUS: Well said! I recognize you as my sons. Listening to you—yes, I heard everything you said—I reproach myself for not talking to you more often. But I want to say first of all—you boys must respect your sisters. The conquest of what lies too close at hand can never be very profitable. To grow up, one must look far beyond oneself. And again: don't always look behind you. Be persuaded that humanity is beyond question much farther from its goal, which we cannot yet glimpse, than from its point of departure, which itself has already vanished from our view.

ETEOCLES: This goal—what can it be?

ŒDIPUS: Whatever it is, it lies before us. I can picture the time, far distant from our own, when the earth will be peopled by a race of men, owing allegiance to no one, who will look back upon our civilization of today as we ourselves look back upon the condition of man at the beginning of his slow progress. If I overcame the Sphinx, it was not so that you should take your ease. The dragon of which you were speaking, Eteocles, is like the one that was waiting for me at the gates of Thebes, where I owed it to myself to enter in triumph. Tiresias bores us with his morality and his mysticism. I had learned all that at Polybius' court—Tiresias has never thought of anything for himself and could never give his approval to those who are all for discovery and invention.

He claims to be inspired by God, with his auguries and revelations, but it wasn't he who
answered the riddle. It was I and I alone who
understood that the only password, if one didn't
want to be eaten alive by the Sphinx, was *Man*.
No doubt it took a certain courage to bring out
that word. But I had it ready even before I heard
the riddle; and my strength was that I would
admit of no other answer, no matter what the
question might be.

You must understand, my boys, that each one
of us encounters at the beginning of his journey
a monster that confronts him with the riddle that
may prevent him from going farther. And although to each one of us, my children, the Sphinx
may put a different question, you must persuade
yourselves that the answer is always the same.
Yes, there is only this one same answer to those
many and various questions; and that this one
answer is: Man; and that this one man, for each
and all of us, is: Oneself.

(*Enter Tiresias.*)

TIRESIAS: Œdipus, is that the last word of your wisdom? Is that where all your knowledge leads?

ŒDIPUS: Not at all. That's where it begins. That is the
first word.

TIRESIAS: And what are the words that come after?

ŒDIPUS: My sons will have to find them.

TIRESIAS: They will not find them, any more than you
yourself have found them.

ŒDIPUS (*aside*): He is more exhausting than the
Sphinx itself. (*to his sons*) Leave us.

(*Exeunt Eteocles and Polynices.*)

TIRESIAS: Yes—you ask your sons to go away when

you have nothing more to tell them and your knowledge has run short. You have nothing but pride to teach them. All knowledge that starts from man, not from God, is worthless.

ŒDIPUS: For a long time I believed myself to be guided by a god.

TIRESIAS: A god who was none other than yourself; yes, yourself deified.

ŒDIPUS: A god (this I learned from you) whom I could do without.

TIRESIAS: That false god, certainly: but not the real God, not the God whom you refuse to know, but who none the less watches your every step and surveys your most secret thoughts: not the God who knows you as you do not know yourself.

ŒDIPUS: What makes you think I do not know my-self?

TIRESIAS: The fact that you think yourself happy.

ŒDIPUS: Why should I not think myself happy, when I am?

TIRESIAS: The invalid who thinks he is well has no great wish to be cured.

ŒDIPUS: Are you trying to convince me that I am ill?

TIRESIAS: Yes, and the more ill for not knowing it. O Œdipus, you try to escape from God, and you don't even know who you are; I should like to teach you to see yourself.

ŒDIPUS: To hear you talk, anybody would think that I was the blind one of us two.

TIRESIAS: If my eyes of flesh are closed, it is so that I can see better with the eyes of the spirit.

ŒDIPUS: And what do you see with the eyes of the spirit?

TIRESIAS: Your miseries. But tell me this: since when

have you ceased to adore God?

ŒDIPUS: Since I began to stay away from His altars.

TIRESIAS: Of course our faith must languish if we neglect our devotions. But why, if you were still a believer, did you stop going to the altars?

ŒDIPUS: Because my hands were no longer clean.

TIRESIAS: With what crime were they sullied?

ŒDIPUS: On the road that was leading me to my consultation with God and my struggle with the Sphinx I committed murder.

TIRESIAS: Whom did you kill?

ŒDIPUS: An unknown man, whose carriage lay across my road.

TIRESIAS: That road was taking you to God. It was not on that road that you met the Sphinx. But you knew that God will not answer those whose hands were sullied.

ŒDIPUS: Quite right—that is why I decided to forfeit His advice, changed my direction, and took the road that led me to the Sphinx.

TIRESIAS: What were you going to ask of God?

ŒDIPUS: To tell me whose son I was. Then suddenly I decided to remain in ignorance.

TIRESIAS: After the murder.

ŒDIPUS: And suddenly I realized that that very ignorance could be the source of my strength.

TIRESIAS: I thought that you always insisted on knowing everything. But just tell me this, Œdipus: before you took your stand on knowing nothing, why were you so anxious to know the answer to that question—the one you were going to put to God?

ŒDIPUS: Because a fortune-teller had predicted that I should . . . Tiresias, you are importunate. I'm not going to answer any more of your questions.

TIRESIAS: That fortune-teller had also predicted to Laius that he would be killed by his own son. Œdipus, Œdipus, foundling and blasphemous ruler that you are! It is in ignorance of your past that you have become sure of yourself. Your happiness is blind. Open your eyes to your misery— God has withdrawn from you the right to be happy.

(*Exit Tiresias.*)

ŒDIPUS: Get out! Get out! As if I had ever sought happiness! It was to escape from it that as a boy of twenty I ran away from Polybius on my toes, with fists clenched. None can say how beautiful was the dawn above Parnassus as I went forward in the dew to hear God's oracle. I had nothing but my own strength to help me, and I didn't yet know who I was, but with all the possibilities of my being I was rich enough. Yes, God's answer— my destiny depended on it, and how glad I was to offer myself to Him! But there is something at this point that I don't quite understand. It's true that up to now I haven't thought about it very much. One must stop to think, and at that time I was in a hurry to be up and doing. . . . When I left the road that was taking me to God, was it really because my hands were no longer pure? I didn't worry about such things then, but now I even think that it was my crime that first sent me off to meet the Sphinx. For what does one look to God? For answers. I felt that I was myself the answer to some as yet unknown question. It was the riddle of the Sphinx, and I was sharp enough to solve it. But since then hasn't everything got

steadily darker before me? Since then, since then—
What have you done, Œdipus? Dulled by my
rewards, I had been twenty years asleep. But
now at last I feel within me the new monster
stirring. A great destiny awaits me, lurking somewhere in the shadows of evening. Œdipus, your
days of tranquillity are over. You must awake
from happiness.

ACT III

I beg you, do not take me for one who despises the laws.

SOPHOCLES:

ŒDIPUS AT COLONUS

ŒDIPUS (*clinging to Jocasta by a fold of her royal robes*): No, no—I insist on knowing. Do not slip away like a shadow. I have not done with you yet. Not till I have every particle of truth, every scrap that you have so far withheld—not till then shall I let you go. There is something crooked in all this; cost what it may, I shall put it straight. First of all, when I entered Thebes after my triumph over the Sphinx, did you already know that Laius was dead?

JOCASTA: How could I promise the throne to the conqueror of the Sphinx before I knew that I was a widow?

ŒDIPUS: Answering the Sphinx's riddle did not in itself win for me the crown of Thebes. The king had also to be killed.

JOCASTA: Of what are you going to accuse yourself?

ŒDIPUS: Not so fast, not so fast. I only mean that Laius had to be dead.

JOCASTA: Listen. I don't really remember what happened, or how long ago it was. . . . Creon must remember. He will tell you.

ŒDIPUS: As if I cared for Creon! Do you know what he has told me already? That I should reward rather than punish the murderer of Laius since, but for his crime, I could never have become king. But tell me now, Jocasta, the death of Laius —you did know about it, didn't you?

JOCASTA: But, my dear, how do you expect me to remember? Why do you torment yourself so? I only know one thing: the moment I saw you, I wanted you.

ŒDIPUS: If I was to have this throne, this bed, they had first to be made empty. Only the king's murder allowed me to have them. But you—you didn't know, then, that you were already free?

JOCASTA: Dear, dear Œdipus, do not call attention to it. None of the historians has noticed yet.

ŒDIPUS: Now I see it all. You knew— The man who killed the king . . .

JOCASTA: Stop!

ŒDIPUS: The man who killed the king was I.

JOCASTA: Not so loud!

ŒDIPUS: When I went to meet the Sphinx I was still sullied with the blood of a man.

JOCASTA: No more, no more!

ŒDIPUS: He wanted to stop me. His carriage barred my road. I picked a quarrel with him, so that he should leave the way free, and I killed him. That unknown man, for all that he wore no crown, was—

JOCASTA: Why must you know?

ŒDIPUS: I need very much to know.

JOCASTA: Have you no pity upon your happiness?

ŒDIPUS: Pity upon nothing. I don't want a happiness made up of blundering ignorance. Good enough for the people, I dare say! For my part, I don't need to be happy. It's all over now! The golden cloud of that enchantment has blown away. You may come in, Tiresias.

(*Enter Tiresias, led by Creon.*)

TIRESIAS: You have need of me?

ŒDIPUS: Not yet. I must first go down to the very bottom of the abyss. This king whom I killed, tell me— No, don't speak. I see it all. I was his son.

CREON: Well, upon my word! What's that I hear? That would make my sister his mother! Œdipus, whom I thought so much of! I can't imagine anything more abominable! Not to know if he's my brother-in-law or my nephew!

ŒDIPUS: Why bother my head with such problems? If my sons are also my brothers, I shall love them the better for it.

CREON: Allow me to say that this confusion of sentiment is most painful to me. Besides, as your uncle, I am entitled to a certain respect.

ŒDIPUS: How hideously am I rewarded for that riddle! So that is what is hidden on the other side of the Sphinx! And for me, who congratulated myself on not knowing my parents! Thanks to which I married my mother—alas! alas!—and with her all my past. I see now why my valor slumbered. In vain did the future call to me. Jocasta drew me backward—Jocasta, who tried in her madness to suppress what had to be, whom I loved as a husband and, all unwittingly, as a son.

. . . Now it is time. Leave me! I am breaking the
cord that binds us. . . . And you, my children,
the companions of my somnolence, the darkened
image of my satisfied desires, it is without you
that I must enter the evening of my life and fulfill
my destiny.

TIRESIAS: Œdipus, son of error and of sin, be born
anew! You needed to suffer to be reborn. Repent!
Come to God, who is waiting for you! Your crime
shall be forgiven.

ŒDIPUS: That crime was imposed by God. His was
the ambush on my road. Before even I was born,
the trap was laid, and I could not but fall into it.
For either your oracle was lying or I had no possible escape. I was caught.

TIRESIAS: Caught by God, who alone can reconcile
you with yourself and wash away your sin. No
other solution is open to you. But should not the
people be told? You yourself have led them to
hope that, in order to deliver them from their misfortunes, the culprit will be punished in accordance with God's decree.

ŒDIPUS: Go, then. Warn whom you please. It is my
wish that all should know. Fetch my children
also. But tell them yourself, tell everyone, what I
myself could never say—tell them of the crime
that I know not how to name.
(*Exit Tiresias.*)

JOCASTA: Why make public what may still be our
own secret? Nobody would have guessed. It's not
yet too late. People have forgotten the crime.
So far from hindering your happiness, it has made
it possible. Nothing has changed.

ŒDIPUS: How can you say nothing has changed? Do you realize that nothing can now reassume, for my lidless eyes, its pristine look of innocence? And besides—I was a king's son without knowing it. I had no need to kill to become a king, but merely to wait.

JOCASTA: The gods decided otherwise.

ŒDIPUS: What I did I had to do. I who thought myself guided by a god! On that belief I founded my confidence in happiness. Later I gave up even that belief in order thenceforward to believe in nothing but myself. But now I no longer recognize myself in my actions. There is one of them, astream with blood, and yet clearly of my own devising, that I should like to disavow—so completely is its aspect altered. Or at any rate I see it now with new eyes, and everything looks different to me.

JOCASTA: A god was blinding you in those days.

ŒDIPUS: God, you say. I felt strong enough to resist even God Himself. I wanted to turn away from Him, when I made off toward the Sphinx. Why? That's what I've come to understand today. I was content to remain subject to God while He led me to glory, but not if He was driving me to commit a crime—and a crime whose horror He hid from me. . . . Oh, most cowardly betrayal of God, no longer to be tolerated. And now am I still God's puppet? Has the oracle foretold what I must do next? Must I still consult it? And find out, O Tiresias, what the birds have to say? . . . If only I could escape from the God who envelops me, escape from myself! Something heroic, something superhuman torments me. I should like to invent some new form of unhappiness—some mad gesture to astonish you all, and astonish myself, and astonish the gods.

(*Exit Œdipus.*)

JOCASTA: Follow him, Creon. Do not leave him alone for a single moment.

(*Exit Creon.*)

O unhappy Œdipus! Why did you have to know? I did what I could to stop you from tearing aside the veil that protected our happiness. Now that you have repulsed me, left me hideously exposed, how can I dare to reappear before you, before our children, before the people whom I hear approaching? . . . If only I could turn back and undo what was done—forget our shameful bed and face the dead who await me as the wife of Laius alone, whom I long to rejoin! . . .

(*Exit Jocasta. Enter Double Chorus.*)

DOUBLE CHORUS (*in antiphony*)

Where's the queen going?	To hide herself, of course!
Where is Œdipus?	He too is hiding. He is ashamed.
Sleeping with his mother and getting her with children in his turn. . . .	All that is family history —no concern of ours.
It concerns the gods, and very annoyed they are.	And then there is the murder of Laius, of which Œdipus, his son, was guilty.

And which Œdipus himself has sworn to avenge.

Ah! He's put himself in a fine mess there, and no mistake.

The judge must arraign himself, and has pointed to himself as the victim.

Doubtless nothing less than a king would have satisfied the gods, so great were our misfortunes.

Besides, it's natural, isn't it, that a king should sacrifice himself for his people?

Yes, if that sacrifice is to deliver us from our woes.

(The Chorus here forms one group.)

CHORUS: O Œdipus, who called yourself happy while yet you were wallowing in infamy, would that we had never known you! You delivered us from the Sphinx, true enough; but your contempt for the gods earned us woes beyond number, which outweigh the benefits we owe you. All happiness won in despite of the gods is happiness falsely acquired; early or late, the gods exact their price. Let us raise our voices in this strain, for here comes Tiresias.

(Enter Tiresias with Œdipus' children.)

TIRESIAS: My children, you know where to seek refuge when a father's protection is withdrawn from you. Hearken to what will shortly precipitate you into life: Œdipus is bound by oath to avenge the death of Laius.

ETEOCLES: He can no longer rule in Thebes.

POLYNICES: He can no longer remain in the country.

ANTIGONE: Do not speak cruel words which the gods can hear and will later turn against you.

ETEOCLES: We shall follow our father's example.

POLYNICES: But we at least shall not need to kill in order to succeed him on the throne.

ANTIGONE: My father did not wittingly commit his crime.

ETEOCLES: We shall have no crime to expiate.

(*Cries within.*)

CHORUS: What shouts are those?

ISMENE: I am afraid.

ANTIGONE: Come close to me.

(*Creon comes out from the palace.*)

CREON: The punishment is more terrible than the crime. Jocasta, your mother, is no more. While I kept watch over Œdipus, she put an end to her life. "What mine eyes should never have beheld" (those were Œdipus' words)—that did I see. I saw my poor sister hanging. Then a moment later, when I was running to help her, Œdipus, running in his turn, snatched up his royal cloak, wrenched off its golden clasps, and plunged them deep into his eyes—most savagely, until their jelly, mixed with blood, bespattered me and streamed across his face. The cries you heard were his—of horror first, and then of grief.

TIRESIAS: We no longer hear them.

CREON: No doubt he has fainted.

CHORUS: No, here he comes, with hesitant step.

(*Leaving Ismene, Antigone throws herself at Œdipus' feet.*)

ANTIGONE: Father—

ŒDIPUS: Is this Antigone whose hair I am touching? Antigone, at once my sister and my daughter. . . .

ANTIGONE: Ah! Do not remind me of that disgrace. I

do not wish to see myself as anything other than your daughter.

ŒDIPUS: You have never lied to me. Tell me, now that I can no longer see for myself, where I may find Tiresias.

ANTIGONE: There, Father, in front of you.

ŒDIPUS: Near enough for him to hear my voice?

TIRESIAS: Yes, I hear you, Œdipus. You wished to speak to me?

ŒDIPUS: Is that what you wanted, Tiresias? In your jealousy of my light, did you seek to drag me into your darkness? I, too, gaze now upon the celestial dark. I have punished these eyes for their failure to guide me thither. No more can you overwhelm me with the superiority of the blind.

TIRESIAS: So it is pride, still pride, that made you dash out your eyes. God did not expect this new forfeit in payment for your early crimes, but merely that you should repent.

ŒDIPUS: Now that I am calmer and I have eased my grief by turning it in exasperation against myself, I can debate with you, Tiresias. I am surprised that this offer of repentance should come from you, who believe that the gods are in complete control of us, and that it was never in my power to escape my destiny. Doubtless my offering of myself was also foreseen, so that I could not but have made it. No matter! Willingly do I sacrifice myself. I had gone so far that I could go farther only by turning in violence against myself.

CREON: I am delighted, my dear Œdipus, to see that, all in all, your griefs are bearable; for it remains for me to give you a rather painful piece of news.

After what has happened, and now that the people know of your crime, you can no longer remain in Thebes.

CHORUS: We ask you, in accordance with the expressed wish of the gods, to disembarrass us at once of your presence and of our woes.

CREON: Eteocles and Polynices already hanker after the throne. If they are perhaps still rather young to reign, I shall once again act as regent.

TIRESIAS: I fancy you will not be astonished to find that your sons have acted upon the teaching that you gave them?

ŒDIPUS: All willingly do I leave them, for their undoing, a kingdom neither won nor deserved. But they have picked out from my example merely what flatters them—authority and license—and let slip what is best and most difficult—self-discipline.

ANTIGONE: Father, I know very well that you will always choose whatever course is noblest. That is why I shall never leave you.

TIRESIAS: You are already promised to God, and cannot dispose of yourself.

ANTIGONE: No, I shall not break my promise. In escaping from you, Tiresias, I shall remain faithful to God. It even seems to me that I shall serve Him better by following my father than I did by being with you. Until today I listened to your interpretation of God; but now, and yet more reverently, I shall listen only to my own heart and mind. Father, lay your hand on my shoulder. I shall not flinch. You can rest on me. I shall clear the briers from your path. Tell me where you want to go.

ŒDIPUS: I don't know. Straight ahead. . . . Henceforward with no roof, no country for my own.

ISMENE: Oh! I can't bear to see you go like this. Just give me time to order a black dress and I'll catch up with you on horseback.

TIRESIAS: Before we let Œdipus go, listen, all of you, to what the gods reveal to me. They promise great blessings to the country in which his bones will rest.

CREON: Well, that's capital! You see how much better you'd do to stay with us. We can always come to some arrangement.

ŒDIPUS: Too late, Creon. My soul is already gone from Thebes, and all that bound me to the past is broken. I am no longer a king; nothing but a nameless traveler who renounces his possessions, his great name, and himself.

CHORUS: Stay with us, Œdipus. We shall look after you well, you'll find. Remember that you once did us great service. If your crimes did put the gods against us, you have taken a master's vengeance upon yourself. Think of your dear Thebans, your people. What can you care for those who do not know you?

ŒDIPUS: Whoever they may be, they are men. I shall be glad to bring them happiness at the price of my sufferings.

TIRESIAS: It is not their happiness that one should seek, but their salvation.

ŒDIPUS: I leave you to explain that to the people. Farewell! Come, my daughter. In you, alone of my children, do I wish to recognize myself. In you I put my trust, unblemished Antigone. You alone shall be my guide.

Theseus

I dedicate this, the latest of my writings, to
ANNE HEURGON
*to whom it belongs by right, for only thanks to her
charming hospitality and her continual
thoughtfulness was I able to complete it.*

I am grateful also to
JACQUES HEURGON
*and to all those who, during a long period of exile,
made it possible for me to understand the full value
of friendship; and particularly to*
JEAN AMROUCHE
*who so greatly encouraged me in a piece of work
that, but for him, I might not have had the
heart to undertake, although it had long been one
of my dreams.*

A. G.

ONE

I WANTED TO TELL the story of my life as a lesson for my son Hippolytus; but he is no more, and I am telling it all the same. For his sake I should not have dared to include, as I shall now do, certain passages of love; he was extraordinarily prudish, and in his company I never dared to speak of my attachments. Besides, these only mattered to me during the first part of my life; but at least they taught me to know myself, as did also the various monsters whom I subdued. For "the first thing is to know exactly who one is," I used to say to Hippolytus; "later comes the time to assess and adopt one's inheritance. Whether you wish it or not, you are, as I was myself, a king's son. Nothing to be done about it; it's a fact; it pins you down." But Hippolytus never took much notice; even less than I had taken at his age; and like myself at that time, he got on very nicely without it. Oh, early years, all innocently passed! Oh, careless growth of body and mind! I was wind; I was wave. I grew with the plant; I flew with the bird. My self knew no boundaries; every contact with an outer world did not so much teach me my own limits as awaken within me some new power of enjoyment. Fruit I caressed, and the bark of young trees, and smooth stones on the shore, and the coats of horses and dogs, before ever my hands were laid on a woman. Toward all the charming things that Pan, Zeus, or Thetis could offer, I rose.

One day my father said to me that things couldn't go on as they were. "Why not?" Because, good heavens, I was his son and must show myself worthy of the throne to which I should succeed. . . . Just when I was feeling so happy, sprawled naked among cool grasses or on some scorching beach. Still, I can't say that he was wrong. Certainly he was right in teaching me to rebel against myself. To this I owe all that I have achieved since that day; no longer to live at random—agreeable as such license might have been. He taught me that nothing great, nothing of value, and nothing that will last can be got without effort.

My first effort was made at his invitation. It was to overturn boulders in the hope of finding the weapons which Poseidon (so he told me) had hidden beneath one of them. He laughed to see how quickly my strength grew through this training. With the toughening of my body there came also a toughening of the will. After I had dislodged the heaviest rocks of the neighborhood and was about to continue my unfruitful search by attacking the flagstones of the palace gateway, my father stopped me. "Weapons," said he, "count for less than the arm that wields them, and the arm in its turn for less than the thinking will that directs it. Here are the weapons. Before giving them to you, I was waiting to see you deserve them. I can sense in you now the ambition to use them, and that longing for fame which will allow you to take up arms only in defense of noble causes and for the weal of all mankind. Your childhood is over. Be a man. Show your fellow men what one of their kind can be and what he means to become. There are great things to be done. Claim yourself."

TWO

ÆGEUS, MY FATHER, was an excellent person; all that could be wished. In point of fact, I suspect that I was his son only in name. That's what I've been told, and that great Poseidon begat me. In which case it's from this god that I inherit my inconstancy of temper. Where women are concerned, I have never known how to settle down. Ægeus sometimes stood rather in my way; but I am grateful to him for his guardianship, and for having restored the cult of Aphrodite to honor in Attica. I am sorry for the fateful slip by which I brought about his death—when I forgot, I mean, to run up white sails in place of black on the ship that carried me home from Crete. It had been agreed that I should do this if I were to return in triumph from my rash venture. One can't think of everything. But to tell the truth, and if I cross-question myself (a thing I never much care to do), I can't swear that it was really forgetfulness. Ægeus was in my way, as I told you, and particularly when, through the potions of the witch Medea, who found him (as, indeed, he found himself) a rather elderly bedfellow, he formed the exasperating idea that a second meridian of enjoyment was his for the asking—thus blocking my career, whereas, after all, it's every man in his turn. Anyway, when he saw those black sails . . . I learned, on returning to Athens, that he had thrown himself into the sea.

No one can deny it. I think I have performed some notable services; I've purged the earth once and for all of a host of tyrants, bandits, and monsters; I've cleaned up certain dangerous byroads on which even the bravest could not venture without a shiver; and I've cleared up the skies in such a way that man, his head less bowed, may be less fearful of their surprises.

One must own that in those days the look of the country was hardly reassuring. Between the scattered townships there were huge stretches of uncultivated waste, crossed only by unreliable tracks. There were the dense forests, the mountainous ravines. At the most dangerous points robber gangs had taken up their positions; these pillaged, killed, or at best held for ransom the traveler, and there were no police to stop them. These incidents combined with the purposeful ferocity of wild beasts and the evil power of the deceitful elements until one could hardly tell, when some foolhardy person came to grief, whether the malignity of the gods had struck him down or merely that of his fellow men. Nor, in the case of such monsters as the Sphinx or the Gorgon who fell to Œdipus or to Bellerophon, could one be sure whether the human strain or the divine was preponderant. Whatever was inexplicable was put on to the gods. Terror and religion were so nearly one that heroism often seemed an impiety. The first and principal victories that man had to win were over the gods.

In a fight, whether with man or with god, it is only by seizing one's adversary's own weapon and turning it against him (as I did with the club of Periphetes, the dark giant of Epidaurus) that one can be sure of final victory.

And as for the thunderbolts of Zeus, I can tell you

that the day will come when man will possess himself of them, as Prometheus possessed himself of fire. Yes, those are decisive victories. But with women, at once my strength and my weakness, I was always having to begin again. I escaped from one, only to fall into the lap of some other; nor did I ever conquer a woman who had not first conquered me. Pirithoüs was right when he told me (ah, how well we used to get on!) that the important thing was never to be unmanned by a woman, as was Hercules in the arms of Omphale. And since I have never been able or wished to live without women, he would say to me, as I darted off on each amorous chase: "Go ahead, but don't get stuck." There was one woman who, ostensibly to safeguard my life, would have bound me to herself by a cord—a thin one, it is true, but a fixed rein none the less. This same woman—but of that, more in due time.

Of them all, Antiope came nearest to catching me. She was queen of the Amazons, and like all her subjects had only one breast; but this in no way impaired her beauty. An accomplished runner and wrestler, she had muscles as firm and sturdy as those of our athletes. I took her on in single combat. In my arms she struggled like a leopard. Disarmed, she brought her teeth and nails into play; enraged by my laughter (for I, too, had no weapons) and because she could not stop herself from loving me. I have never possessed anyone more virginal. And little did it matter to me that later she could only suckle my Hippolytus, her son, with one breast. It was this chaste and savage being whom I wished to make my heir. I shall speak, during the course of my story, of what has been the greatest grief of my life. For it is

not enough to exist, and then to have existed: one
must make one's legacy and act in such a way that
one is not extinguished with oneself, so my grand-
father had often told me. Pittheus and Ægeus were
much more intelligent than I; so is Pirithoüs. But
people give me credit for good sense; the rest is
added with the determination to do well that has
never left me. Mine, too, is the kind of courage that
incites me to desperate enterprises. On top of all this
I was ambitious. The great deeds of my cousin
Hercules, which they used to report to me, ex-
asperated my young blood, and when it was time to
leave Troezen, where I had lived till then, and rejoin
my so-called father in Athens, I refused altogether to
accept the advice, sound though it was, to go by sea
because that route was the safer. Well I knew it; but
it was the very hazards of the overland route, with
its immense detour, that tempted me; a chance to
prove my worth. Thieves of every sort were beginning
once again to infest the country, and did so with
impunity now that Hercules was squandering his manhood at the feet of Omphale. I was sixteen. All the
cards were in my hand. My turn had come. In great
leaps my heart was bounding toward the extremity
of my happiness. "What have I to do with safety," I
cried, "and a route that's set in order!" I despised
comfort and idleness and unlaureled ease. So it was
on the road to Athens by way of the isthmus of the
Peloponnesus that I first put myself to the test, and
my heart and my arm together taught me their full
strength, when I cut down some well-known and well-
hated robbers: Sinis, Periphetes, Procrustes, Geryon
(no, that was Hercules; I meant to say Cercyon). By
the way, I made a slight mistake at that time, when

Sciron was concerned, for he turned out afterwards to have been a very worthy man, good-natured and most helpful to passing travelers. But as I had just done away with him, it was soon agreed that he had been a rascal.

Also on the road to Athens, in a thicket of asparagus, there smiled upon me the first of my conquests in love. Perigone was tall and supple. I had just killed her father, and by way of amends I got her a very handsome son: Menalippes. I have lost track of both of them—breaking free, as usual, and anxious never to lose any time. I have never allowed the past to involve or detain me; rather have I been drawn forward by what was still to be achieved; and the most important things seemed to me always to lie ahead.

So much so that I won't waste more time with these preliminary trifles, which, after all, meant only too little to me. Here I was on the threshold of an admirable adventure. Hercules himself never had one like it. I must tell it at length.

THREE

IT'S VERY COMPLICATED, this story. I must say first that the island of Crete was a power in those days. Minos reigned there. He held Attica responsible for the death of his son Androgeus; and by way of reprisal he had exacted from us an annual tribute: seven young men and seven young girls had to be handed over to satisfy, it was said, the appetites of the Minotaur, the monstrous child that Pasiphaë, the wife of Minos, had brought forth after intercourse with a bull. These victims were chosen by lot.

But in the year in question, I had just returned to Greece. Though the lot would normally have spared me (princes readily escape these things), I insisted that I should figure in the list, notwithstanding the opposition of the king, my father. I care nothing for privilege, and claim that merit alone distinguishes me from the herd. My plan was, in point of fact, to vanquish the Minotaur and thus at a blow to free Greece from this abominable exaction. Also I was most anxious to visit Crete, whence beautiful, costly, and unusual objects were constantly arriving in Attica. Therefore I set sail for the island; among my thirteen companions was my friend Pirithoüs.

We landed, one morning in March, at Amnisos, a little township that served as harbor to its neighbor Knossos, the capital of the island, where Minos resided and had had his palace built. We should have arrived the previous evening, but a violent storm had delayed us. As we stepped ashore we were surrounded by armed guards, who took away my sword and that of Pirithoüs. When they had searched us for other weapons, they led us off to appear before the king, who had come from Knossos, with his court, to meet us. A large crowd of the common people pressed round to have a look at us. All the men were naked to the waist except Minos, who, seated beneath a dais, wore a long robe made from a single piece of dark-red cloth; this fell in majestic folds from his shoulders to his ankles. His chest, broad as that of Zeus himself, bore three tiers of necklaces. Many Cretans wear these, but of a trumpery sort. Minos had necklaces of rare stones, and plaques of wrought gold in the shape of fleurs-de-lis. The double-headed ax hung above his throne, and with his right hand he stretched before him a golden scepter, as tall as himself. In the other hand was a three-leaved flower, like those on his neck-laces, and also in gold, but larger. Above his golden crown was a gigantic panache, in which were mingled the feathers of peacock, ostrich, and halcyon. He looked us over for some time and then bade us wel-come to the island, with a smile that may well have been ironical, since we had come there, after all, under sentence of death. By his side were standing the queen and the two princesses, her daughters. I saw at once that the elder daughter had taken a fancy to me. As our guards were making ready to take us away, I saw her lean toward her father and say to him in Greek (she whispered, but my ears are sharp): "Not that one, I beg you," and she pointed toward me with her finger. Minos smiled once again and gave orders that I should not be taken away with my companions.

I was no sooner alone before him than he began to question me.

Although I had promised myself to act with all possible prudence and to let slip no hint either of my noble birth or of my audacious project, it suddenly occurred to me that it would be better to put my cards on the table, now that I had attracted the attention of the princess. Nothing would be more likely to heighten her feeling for me, or to win me the favor of the king, than to hear me say frankly that I was the grandson of Pittheus. I even hinted that the current rumor in Attica was that the great Poseidon had begot me. To this Minos replied gravely that he would presently clear up that point by submitting me to trial by water. In return I replied complacently that I had no doubt I should survive triumphantly any test that he cared to impose. The ladies of the court, if not Minos himself, were favorably affected by my self-confidence.

"And now," said Minos, "you must go and have something to eat. Your companions are already at table and will be waiting for you. After such a disturbed night you must be quite peckish, as they say here. Have a good rest. I shall expect you to be present toward the end of the day at the ceremonial games in honor of your visit. Then, Prince Theseus, we shall take you with us to Knossos. You will sleep at the palace, and tomorrow evening you will dine with us —a simple, family meal, where you will feel quite at home, and these ladies will be delighted to hear you tell of your first exploits. And now they are going to prepare themselves for the festivities. We shall meet again at the games, where you will sit, with your companions, immediately beneath the royal box. This courtesy we owe to your princely rank; and as I do not wish to distinguish you openly from your companions they shall, by contagion, rank with you."

The games were held in a vast semicircular arena, opening on the sea. Huge crowds, both of men and of women, had come to see them, from Knossos, from Lyttos, and even from Gortyna (a matter of two hundred stadia distant, I was told), from other towns and their neighboring villages, and from the thickly populated open country. All my senses were taken by surprise, and I cannot describe how foreign the Cretans appeared to me to be. As there was not room for them all on the tiers of the amphitheater, they pushed and jostled their way up the staircases and along the aisles. The women, no less numerous than the men, were for the most part naked to the waist. A very few wore a light bodice, but even this was generously cut away, in a fashion that I could not help thinking rather immodest, and exposed both breasts to the air. Men and women alike were tightly, even absurdly laced around the hips with belts and corselets, which gave to each the figure of an hourglass. The men were nearly all brown-skinned, and at their fingers, wrists, and throats wore almost as many rings, bracelets, and necklaces as the women, who, for their part, were perfectly white. All the men were clean-shaven, except for the king, Rhadamanthus, his brother, and his friend Dædalus. The ladies of the court sat on a platform just above our own, which dominated the arena from a considerable height. They had indulged a prodigious extravagance of dress and ornament. Each wore a flounced skirt; billowing out oddly below the hips, this fell in embroidered

furbelows to their feet, which were shod in little boots
of white leather. The fatuosity of the queen, who sat
in the center of the dais, made her most conspicuous
of all. Her arms and the front of her person were bare.
Upon her magnificent breasts, pearls, emeralds, and
precious stones were embanked. Long black curls fell
on either side of her face, and smaller ringlets
streaked her forehead. She had the lips of a glutton,
an upturned nose, and huge empty eyes, whose ex-
pression one might have called bovine. A sort of
golden diadem served her as a crown. It sat, not
directly on her hair, but on a ridiculous hat of some
dark material, which came up through the diadem and
tapered into a sharp point, like a horn, which jutted
far out in front of her forehead. Her corsage un-
covered her to the waist in front, but rose high at the
back and ended in an enormous cutaway collar. Her
skirt was spread wide around her, and one could
admire, upon their creamy ground, three rows of
embroidery, one above the other—purple irises at the
top, saffrons in the center, and below them violets
with their leaves. As I was sitting immediately below,
I had only to turn round to have all this, as one might
say, under my very nose. I marveled as much at the
sense of color and the beauty of the design as at the
delicate perfection of the work.

Ariadne, the elder daughter, sat at her mother's
right hand and presided over the corrida. She was
less sumptuously dressed than the queen, and she wore
different colors. Her skirt, like that of her sister, had
only two circles of embroidery: on the upper one,
dogs and hinds; on the lower, dogs and partridges.
Phædra, perceptibly a much younger girl, sat on
Pasiphaë's left. Her dress had a frieze of children

running after hoops, and another of younger children squatting on their behinds and playing marbles. She took a childish pleasure in the spectacle. As for me, I could hardly follow what was going on, it was all so disconcertingly new; but I could not help being amazed by the suppleness, speed, and agility of the acrobats who took their chance in the arena after the singers, the dancers, and then the wrestlers had had their turn. Myself about to encounter the Minotaur, I learned a good deal from watching the feints and passes that might help me to baffle and tire the bull.

FOUR

After ariadne had rewarded the last champion with the last prize, Minos declared the games closed. Escorted by his courtiers, he bade me come to him separately.

"I am going to take you now, Prince Theseus," he said to me, "to a place by the sea where I shall put you to the test, and we shall see if you are the true son of the god Poseidon, as you claimed to be just now."

He took me to a small promontory with waves beating at its foot. "I shall now," said the king, "throw my crown into the sea, as a mark of my confidence that you will be able to retrieve it from the bottom."

The queen and the two princesses were there to see what would come of the test; and so, emboldened by their presence, I protested:

"Am I a dog, to fetch and carry for my master, even if it be a crown? Let me dive in without bait and I shall bring back to you something or other that will attest and prove my case."

In my audacity I went still farther. A stiff breeze had sprung up, and it happened that a long scarf was dislodged from Ariadne's shoulders. A gust blew it toward me. I caught it with a smile, as if the princess or one of the gods had offered it to me. Then, stripping off my close-fitting corselet, I wrapped the scarf round my loins in its place, twisted it up between my thighs, and made it fast. It looked as if I did this from modesty, lest I should expose my manhood before these ladies; but in fact it allowed me to hide the leather belt that I was still wearing, to which was attached a small purse. In this I had, not metal coins, but some valuable stones that I had brought with me from Greece, knowing that they would keep their full value, no matter where I went.

Then I took a deep breath and dived.

A practiced swimmer, I dived deep, and did not come up to the surface until I had removed from my purse an onyx and two chrysoprases. Once back on dry land I offered, with my most chivalrous bow, the onyx to the queen and a chrysoprase to each of her daughters. I pretended to have gathered them on the bottom, or rather (since it was hardly plausible that the stones, so rare upon dry land, should have lain promiscuously at the bottom of the sea, or that I should have had time to pick them out) that Poseidon himself had handed them to me, in order that I could offer them to the ladies. Here was proof, better than any test, of my divine origin and my good standing with the god.

After this, Minos gave me back my sword.

Soon afterwards chariots bore us off on the road to Knossos.

FIVE

I WAS SO OVERWHELMED by fatigue that I could hardly feel due astonishment at the great courtyard of the palace, or at a monumental balustraded staircase and the winding corridors through which attentive servants, torch in hand, guided me to the second floor, where a room had been set apart for me. All but one of its many lamps were snuffed out after I arrived. The bed was scented and soft; when they left me, I fell at once into a heavy sleep, which lasted until the evening of the following day, although I had already slept during our long journey; for only at dawn, after traveling all night, had we arrived at Knossos.

I am by no means a cosmopolitan. At the court of Minos I realized for the first time that I was Greek, and I felt very far from home. All unfamiliar things took me by surprise—dress, customs, ways of behaving, furniture (in my father's house we were short of furniture), household objects, and the manner of their use. Among so much that was exquisite, I felt like a savage, and my awkwardness was redoubled when people began smiling at my conduct. I had been used to biting my way through my food, lifting it to my mouth in my fingers, and these delicate forks of metal or wrought gold, these knives they used for cutting meat, gave me more trouble than the heaviest weapons of war. People couldn't take their eyes off me; and when I had to talk, I appeared a still greater oaf.

God! How out of place I felt! Only on my own have I ever been good for anything; now for the first time I was in society. It was no longer a question of fighting, or carrying a thing through by main force, but rather of giving pleasure; and of this I had strangely little experience.

I sat, at table, between the two princesses. A simple family meal, without formality, I was told. And in fact, apart from Minos and the queen, Rhadamanthus, the king's brother, the two princesses, and their young brother Glaucus, there was nobody except the tutor to the young prince, a Greek from Corinth, who was not even presented to me.

They asked me to describe in my own tongue (which everybody at the court understood very well and spoke fluently, though with a slight accent) what they were pleased to call my exploits. I was delighted to see that the young Phædra and Glaucus were seized with uncontrollable laughter at the story of the treatment that Procrustes imposed upon passers-by, which I made him endure in his turn—chopping off all those parts of him which exceeded his statutory measure. But they tactfully avoided any allusion to the cause of my visit to Crete, and affected to see me as merely a traveler.

Throughout the meal Ariadne pressed her knee against mine under the table; but it was the warmth of the young Phædra that really stirred me. Meanwhile, Pasiphaë, the queen, who sat opposite me, was fairly eating me with her enormous eyes, and Minos, by her side, wore an unvarying smile. Only Rhadamanthus, with his long, fair beard, seemed rather out of humor. Both he and the king left the room after

the fourth course—"to sit on their thrones," they said.
Only later did I realize what this meant.

I still felt some traces of my seasickness. I ate a
great deal, and drank still more. I was so liberally
plied with wines and liqueurs of every sort that before
long I didn't know where I was. I was used to drinking only water or diluted wine. With everything reel-
ing before me, but still just able to stand, I begged
permission to leave the room. The queen at once led
me into a small closet that adjoined her private apart-
ments. After I had been thoroughly sick, I rejoined her
on a sofa in her room, and it was then that she began
to tackle me.

"My young friend—if I may call you so," she began,
"we must make the most of these few moments alone
together. I am not what you suppose, and have no
designs upon your person, attractive as that may be."
And, protesting the while that she was addressing herself only to my spirit, or to some undefined but in-
terior zone of my being, she continually stroked my
forehead; later she slipped her hands under my leather
jerkin and fondled my pectorals, as if to convince herself that I was really there.

"I know what brings you here, and I want to warn
you of a mistake. Your intentions are murderous. You
are here to fight my son. I don't know what you may
have heard about him, and I don't want to know. Ah,
listen to the pleas of my heart! He whom they call the
Minotaur may or may not be the monster of whom
you have no doubt heard, but he is my son."

At this point I thought it only decent to interject
that I had nothing against monsters in themselves;
but she went on without listening.

"Please try to understand me. By temperament I am a mystic. Heavenly things alone excite my love. The difficulty, you see, is one never can tell exactly where the god begins and where he ends. I have seen a good deal of my cousin Leda. For her the god hid himself in the guise of a swan. Now, Minos always knew that I wanted to give him a Dioscuros for his heir. But how can one distinguish the animal residue that may remain even in the seed of the gods? If I have since then deplored my mistake—and I realize that to talk of it in this way robs the affair of all grandeur—yet I assure you, Theseus, that it was a celestial moment. For you must understand that my bull was no ordinary beast. Poseidon had sent him. He should have been offered to him as a sacrifice, but he was so beautiful that Minos could not bring himself to do it. That is how I have been able ever since to pass off my desires as an instrument of the god's revenge. And you no doubt know that my mother-in-law, Europa, was carried off by a bull. Zeus was hiding inside him. Minos himself was the fruit of their union. That is why bulls have always been held in great honor in his family. And, if ever, after the birth of the Minotaur, I noticed the king knitting his brows, I had only to say: 'What about your mother?' He could only admit that it was a natural mistake. He is very wise. He believes that Zeus has nominated him judge, along with Rhadamanthus, his brother. He takes the view that one must have understood before one can pass judgment, and he thinks that he will not be a good judge until he has experienced everything, either in his own person or through his family. This is a great encouragement for us all. His children, and I myself, in our several ways, are working, by our individual

errors of conduct, for the advancement of his career.
The Minotaur too, though he doesn't know it. That is
why I am begging you here and now, Theseus, not to
try to do him any sort of injury, but rather to become
intimate with him, and so to end a misunderstanding
that has made Crete the enemy of Greece and done
great harm to our two countries."

So saying, she became even more attentive, and a
point was reached at which I was seriously incom-
moded, while the exhalations of wine heightened and
mingled with the powerful effluvium which, in company with her breasts, was escaping from her corsage.

"Let us return to celestial things," she went on, "as
return we always must. You yourself, Theseus—surely
you must feel that you are inhabited by one of the
gods?"

What put the final touch to my embarrassment was
that Ariadne, the elder daughter (and an exceptional
beauty, though less attractive to me personally than
Phædra), had made it quite plain to me, before I
began to feel so sick—had made it quite plain, as I
say, as much by signs as by a whisper, that as soon as
I felt better I was to join her on the terrace.

SIX

WHAT A TERRACE! And what a palace! Trance-like
under the moon, the gardens seemed to be suspended
in readiness for one knew not what. It was the month
of March, but I could sense already the delicious half-
warmth of spring. Once in the open air, I began to
feel quite well. Never an indoor man, I need to fill my
lungs with fresh air. Ariadne came running toward
me, and without a word clamped her warm lips to
mine—so violently that we were both sent staggering.

"Follow me," she said. "Not that I mind if anyone
sees us; but we can talk more freely under the
terebinths." She led me down a few steps toward a
more leafy part of the gardens, where huge trees
obscured the moon, though not its reflection upon the
sea. She had changed her clothes, and now wore, in
place of her hooped skirt and tight surcoat, a sort of
loose dress, beneath which she was palpably naked.

"I can guess what my mother's been telling you,"
she began. "She's mad, raving mad, and you can dis-
regard everything she says. First of all, I must tell
this: you are in great danger here. You came here, as
I well know, to fight my half-brother, the Minotaur.
I'm telling you all this for your own good, so listen
carefully. You will win—I'm sure of it. To see you is
to banish doubt. (Don't you think that's rather a good
line of poetry? But perhaps you have no ear.) But
nobody to this day has ever managed to get out of the

maze in which the monster lives; and you won't succeed either unless your sweetheart (that I am, or shall presently be) comes to your rescue. You can't begin to conceive how complicated it is, that maze. Tomorrow I shall introduce you to Dædalus, who will tell you about it. It was he who built it; but even he has already forgotten how to get out of it. You'll hear from him how his son Icarus, who once ventured inside, could only get out on wings, through the upper air. That I don't dare recommend to you; it's too risky. You'd better get it into your head at once that your only hope is to stick close to me. We shall be together, you and I—we *must* be together, from now on, in life and in death. Only thanks to me, by me, and in me will you be able to recapture yourself. You must take it or leave it. If you leave me, so much the worse for you. So begin by taking me." Whereupon she abandoned all restraint, gave herself freely to my embrace, and kept me in her arms till morning.

The hours passed slowly for me, I must admit. I have never been good at staying in one place, be it even in the very bosom of delight. I always aim to break free as soon as the novelty has worn off. Afterwards Ariadne used to say: "You promised." I never gave a promise of any kind. Liberty above all things! My duty is to myself.

Although my powers of observation were still to some extent clouded by drink, Ariadne appeared to me to yield her last reserves with such readiness that I could hardly suppose myself to have done the work of a pioneer. This disposed of any scruples that I might later have had about leaving her. Besides, her sentimentality soon became unendurable. Unendurable her protestations of eternal devotion, and the

tender diminutives with which she ornamented me. I
was alternately her only treasure, her canary, her
puppy, her tercelet, her guinea fowl. I loathe pet
names. And then she had read too much. "Little
heart," she would say, "the irises will wither fast and
die." (In point of fact, they'd hardly begun to flower.)
I know quite well that nothing lasts forever; but the
present is all that matters to me. And then she would
say: "I couldn't exist without you." This made me
think all the time of how to get rid of her.

"What will the king, your father, say to that?" I had
asked her. And her reply: "Minos, sweet chuck, puts
up with everything. He thinks it's wisest to allow what
cannot be prevented. He didn't complain of my
mother's adventure with the bull, but according to my
mother he simply remarked: 'Here I have some difficulty in following you.' 'What's done is done, and
nothing can undo it,' he added. When it comes to us,
he'll do the same. At the most, he'll banish you from
the court—and a lot of difference that'll make! Wher-
ever you go, I shall follow."

That remains to be seen, I thought.

After we had taken a light breakfast, I asked her to
be kind enough to lead me to Dædalus, and added
that I wished to speak to him privately and alone. She
agreed to this only after I had sworn by Poseidon that
immediately our talk was over, I would rejoin her at
the palace.

SEVEN

DÆDALUS ROSE to welcome me. I had found him in a dim-lit room, bending over the tablets and working drawings that were spread before him, and surrounded by a great many peculiar instruments. He was very tall, and perfectly erect in spite of his great age. His beard was silvery in color, and even longer than that of Minos, which was still quite black, or the fairer one of Rhadamanthus. His vast forehead was marked by deep wrinkles across the whole of its width. When he looked downwards, his eyes were half-hidden by the overhanging brushwood of his eyebrows. He spoke slowly, and in a deep voice. His silences had the quality of thought.

He began by congratulating me on my prowess. The echo of this, he said, had penetrated even to him, who lived in retirement, remote from the tumult of the world. He added that I looked to him to be something of a booby; that he took little account of feats of arms, and did not consider that physical strength was the godhead of man.

"At one time I saw quite a lot of your predecessor Hercules. He was a stupid man, and I could never get anything out of him except heroics. But what I did appreciate in him, and what I appreciate in you, is a sort of absorption in the task in hand, an unrecoiling audacity, a temerity even, which thrusts you forward and destroys your opponent, after first having destroyed the coward whom each of us carries within himself. Hercules took greater pains than you do; was more anxious, also, to do well; rather melancholy, especially when he had just completed an adventure. But what I like in you is your enjoyment; that is where you differ from Hercules. I shall commend you for never letting your mind interfere. You can leave that to others who are not men of action, but are clever at inventing sound and good motives for those who are.

"Do you realize that we are cousins? I too (but don't repeat this to Minos, who knows nothing about it)—I too am Greek. I was forced regretfully to leave Attica after certain differences had arisen between myself and my nephew Talos, a sculptor like myself, and my rival. He became a popular favorite, and claimed to uphold the dignity of the gods by representing them with their lower limbs set fast in a hieratic posture, and thus incapable of movement; whereas I was for setting free their limbs and bringing the gods nearer to ourselves. Olympus, thanks to me, became once again a neighbor of the earth. By way of complement, I aspired, with the aid of science, to mold mankind in the likeness of the gods.

"At your age I longed above all to acquire knowledge. I soon decided that man's personal strength can effect little or nothing without instruments, and that the old saying 'Better a good tool than a strong forearm' was true. Assuredly you could never have subdued the bandits of Attica and the Peloponnese without the weapons your father had given you. So I thought I could not employ myself more usefully than by bringing these auxiliaries nearer to perfection, and that I could not do this without first mastering mathematics, mechanics, and geometry to the degree, at any rate, in which they were known in Egypt, where such things are put to great use; also that I must then pass from theory to practice by learning all that was known about the properties and qualities of every kind of material, even of those for which no immediate use was apparent, for in these (as happens also in the human sphere) one sometimes discovers extraordinary qualities one had never expected to find. And so I widened and entrenched my knowledge.

"To familiarize myself with other trades, other crafts and skills, other climates, and other living things, I set myself to visit distant countries, put myself to school with eminent foreigners, and remained with them until they had nothing more to teach me. But no matter where I went or how long I stayed, I remained a Greek. In the same way it is because I know and feel that you are a son of Greece that I am interested in you, my cousin.

"Once back in Crete, I told Minos all about my studies and my travels, and went on to tell him of a project I had cherished. This was to build and equip, not far from his palace (if he approved the plan and would provide the means to carry it out), a labyrinth like the one which I had admired in Egypt, on the shore of Lake Moeris; but mine would be different in plan. At the very moment Minos was in an awkward position. His queen had whelped a monster; not knowing how best to look after it, but judging it prudent to isolate it and keep it well away from the public gaze, he asked me to devise a building and a set of communicating gardens which, without precisely imprisoning the monster, would at least contain him and make it impossible for him to get loose. I lavished all my scholarship, all my best thoughts, on the task.

"But, believing that no prison can withstand a really obstinate intention to escape, and that there is no barrier, no ditch, that daring and resolution will not overcome, I thought that the best way of containing a prisoner in the labyrinth was to make it of such a kind, not that he couldn't get out (try to grasp my meaning here), but that he wouldn't want to get out. I therefore assembled in this one place the means to satisfy every kind of appetite. The Minotaur's tastes were neither many nor various; but we had to plan for everybody, whomsoever it might be, who would enter the labyrinth. Another and indeed the prime necessity was to fine down the visitor's will-power to the point of extinction. To this end I made up some electuaries and had them mixed with the wines that were served. But that was not enough; I found a better way. I had noticed that certain plants, when thrown into the fire, gave off, as they burned, semi-narcotic vapors. These seemed admirably suited to my purpose, and indeed they played exactly the part for which I needed them. Accordingly I had them fed to the stoves, which are kept alight night and day. The heavy gases thus distributed not only act upon the will and put it to sleep; they induce a delicious intoxication, rich in flattering delusions, and provoke the mind, filled as this is with voluptuous mirages, to a certain pointless activity; 'pointless,' I say, because it has merely an imaginary outcome, in visions and speculations without order, logic, or substance. The effect of these gases is not the same for all of those who breathe them; each is led on by the complexities implicit in his own mind to lose himself, if I may so put it, in a labyrinth of his own devising. For my son Icarus, the complexities were metaphysical. For me, they take the form of enormous

edifices, palatial buildings heaped upon themselves
with an elaboration of corridors and staircases . . .
in which (as with my son's speculations) everything
leads to a blank wall, a mysterious 'keep out.' But the
most surprising thing about these perfumes is that
when one has inhaled them for a certain time, they are
already indispensable; body and mind have formed a
taste for this malicious insobriety; outside of it reality
seems charmless and one no longer has any wish to
return to it. And that—that above all—is what keeps
one inside the labyrinth. Knowing that you want to
enter it in order to fight the Minotaur, I give you fair
warning; and if I have told you at length of this
danger, it was to put you on your guard. You will
never bring it off alone; Ariadne must go with you.
But she must remain on the threshold and not so much
as sniff the vapors. It is important that she should keep
a clear head while you are being overcome by drunkenness. But even when drunk, you must keep control
of yourself: everything depends on that. Your will
alone may not suffice (for, as I told you, these emana-
tions will weaken it), and so I have thought of this
plan: to link you and Ariadne by a thread, the
tangible symbol of duty. This thread will allow, indeed will compel you to rejoin her after you have been
some time away. Be always determined not to break it,
no matter what may be the charms of the labyrinth,
the seduction of the unknown, or the headlong urging
of your own courage. Go back to her, or all the rest,
and the best with it, will be lost. This thread will be
your link with the past. Go back to it. Go back to
yourself. For nothing can begin from nothing, and it
is from your past, and from what you are at this
moment, that what you are going to be must spring.

"I should have spoken more briefly if I had not been so interested in you. But before you go out to meet your destiny, I want you to hear my son. You will realize more vividly, while listening to him, what danger you will presently run. Although he was able, thanks to me, to escape the witchcraft of the maze, his mind is still most pitiably a slave to its maleficence."

He walked over to a small door, lifted the arras that covered it, and said very loudly:

"Icarus, my dear son, come and tell us of your distress. Or, rather, go on thinking aloud, as if you were alone. Pay no attention to me or to my guest. Behave as if neither of us were here."

EIGHT

I saw coming in a young man of about my own age who seemed in the half-light to be of great beauty. His fair hair was worn very long and fell in ringlets to his shoulders. He stared fixedly, but seemed not to focus his gaze on anything in particular. Naked to the waist, he wore a tight metal belt and a loincloth, as it seemed to me, of leather and dark cloth; this swathed the top of his thighs, and was held in place by a curious and prominent knot. His white leather boots caught my eye, and seemed to suggest that he was making ready to go out; but his mind alone was on the move. Himself seemed not to see us. Proceeding no doubt with some unbroken chain of argument, he was saying:

"Who came first: man or woman? Can the Eternal One be female? From the womb of what great Mother have you come, all you myriad species? And by what engendering cause can that womb have been made great? Duality is inadmissible. In that case the god himself would be the son. My mind refuses to divide God. If once I allow division, strife begins. Where there are gods, there are wars. There are not gods, but a God. The kingdom of God is peace. All is absorbed, all is reconciled in the Unique Being."

He was silent for a moment and then went on:

"If man is to give a form to the gods, he must localize and reduce. God spreads where he will. The gods are divided. His extension is immense; theirs merely local."

He was silent again, before going on in a voice panting with anguish:

"But what is the reason for all this, O God who art lucidity itself? For so much trouble, so many struggles? And toward what? What is our purpose here? Why do we seek reasons for everything? Where are we to turn, if not toward God? How are we to direct our steps? Where are we to stop? When can we say: so be it; nothing more to be done? How can we reach God, after starting from man? And if I start from God, how can I reach across to myself? Yet if man is the creation of God, is not God the creation of man? It is at the exact crossing-place of those roads, at the very heart of that cross, that my mind would fix itself."

As he spoke, the veins swelled on his forehead, and the sweat ran down his temples. At least, so it seemed to me, for I could not see him clearly in the half-light; but I heard him gasping, like a man putting forth an immense effort.

He was quiet for a moment, then went on:

"I don't know where God begins, and still less where He ends. I shall even express myself more exactly if I say that His beginning never ends. Ah, how sick I am of 'therefore,' and 'since,' and 'because'! Sick of inference, sick of deduction. I never learn anything from the finest of syllogisms that I haven't first put into it myself. If I put God in at the beginning, He comes out at the end. I don't find Him unless I do put Him in. I have tramped all the roads of logic. On their horizontal plane I have wandered all too often. I crawl, and I would rather take wings; to lose my shadow, to lose the filth of my body, to throw off

the weight of the past! The infinite calls me! I have
the sensation of being drawn upwards from a great
height. O mind of man, I shall climb to your topmost
point. My father, with his great knowledge of mechanics, will provide me with the means to go. I shall
travel alone. I'm not afraid. I can pay my way. It's my
only chance to escape. O noble mind, too long en-
tangled in the confusion of my problems, an un-
charted road is waiting for you now. I cannot define
what it is that summons me; but I know that my
journey can have only one end: in God."

Then he backed away from us as far as the arras,
which he raised and afterwards let drop behind him.

"Poor dear boy," said Dædalus. "As he thought he
could never escape from the labyrinth and did not
understand that the labyrinth was within himself, at
his request I made him a set of wings, with which he
was able to fly away. He thought that he could only
escape by way of the heavens, all terrestrial routes
being blocked. I knew him to be of a mystical turn,
so that his longing did not surprise me. A longing that
has not been fulfilled, as you will have been able to
judge for yourself while listening to him. In spite of
my warnings, he tried to fly too high and overtaxed his
strength. He fell into the sea. He is dead."

"How can that be?" I burst out. "I saw him alive
only a moment ago."

"Yes," he answered, "you did see him, and he
seemed to be alive. But he is dead. At this point,
Theseus, I am afraid that your intelligence, although
Greek, and as such subtle and open to all aspects of
the truth, cannot follow me; for I myself, I must
confess, was slow to grasp and concede this fact:
those of us whose souls, when weighed in the supreme

scale, are not judged of too little account, do not just live an ordinary life. In time, as we mortals measure it, we grow up, accomplish our destiny, and die. But there is another, truer, eternal plane on which time does not exist; on this plane the representative gestures of our race are inscribed, each according to its particular significance. Icarus was, before his birth, and remains after his death, the image of man's disquiet, of the impulse to discovery, the soaring flight of poetry—the things of which, during his short life, he was the incarnation. He played out his hand, as he owed it to himself to do; but he didn't end there. What happens, in the case of a hero, is this: his mark endures. Poetry and the arts reanimate it, and it becomes an enduring symbol. That is how it is that Orion, the hunter, is riding still, across Elysian fields of asphodel, in search of the prey that he has already killed during his life; and meanwhile the night sky bears the eternal, constellated image of him and his baldric. That is how Tantalus' throat is parched to all eternity, and how Sisyphus still rolls upward toward an unattainable summit the heavy and ever rebounding weight of care that tormented him in the days when he was king of Corinth. For you must realize that in hell the only punishment is to begin over and over again the actions which, in life, one failed to complete.

"In the same way, in the animal kingdom, the death of each creature in no way impoverishes its species, for this retains its habitual shape and behavior; there are no individuals among the beasts. Whereas among men it is the individual alone who counts. That is why Minos is already leading at Knossos the life which will fit him for his career as a judge in hell. That is why

Pasiphaë and Ariadne are yielding to their destiny in such exemplary fashion. And you yourself, Theseus, may appear carefree, and you may feel it, but you will not escape the destiny that is shaping you, any more than did Hercules, or Jason, or Perseus. But know this (because my eyes have learned the art of discerning the future through the present)—there remain great things for you to do, and in a sphere quite different from that of your previous exploits; things beside which these exploits will seem, in the future, to have been the amusements of a child. It remains for you to found the city of Athens, and there to situate the supremacy of the human mind.

"Do not linger, therefore, in the labyrinth, or in the embrace of Ariadne, after the hideous combat from which you will emerge triumphant. Keep on the move. Regard indolence as treachery. Seek no rest until, with your destiny completed, it is time to die. It is only thus that, on the farther side of what seems to be death, you will live, forever re-created by the gratitude of mankind. Keep on the move, keep well ahead, keep on your own road, O valiant gatherer of cities.

"And now listen carefully, Theseus, and remember what I say. No doubt you will have an easy victory over the Minotaur. Taken in the right way, he is not so redoubtable as people suppose. (They used to say that he lived on carrion; but since when has a bull eaten anything but grass?) Nothing is easier than to get into the labyrinth, nothing less easy than to get out. Nobody finds his way in there without first he lose it. And for your return journey (for footsteps leave no trace in the labyrinth) you must attach yourself to Ariadne by a thread. I have prepared several reels of this, and you will take them away with you. Unwind them as you make your way inside, and when the reel is exhausted, tie the end of the thread to the beginning of the next, so as never to have a break in the chain. Then on your way back you must rewind the thread until you come to the end, which Ariadne will have in her hand. I don't know why I insist so much, when all that part is as easy as good-morning. The real difficulty is to preserve unbroken, to the last inch of the thread, the will to come back; for the perfumes will make you forgetful, as will also your natural curiosity, which will conspire to make you weaken. I have told you this already and have nothing to add. Here are the reels. Good-by."

I left Dædalus and made off to rejoin Ariadne.

NINE

THOSE REELS OF THREAD were the occasion of the first
dispute between Ariadne and myself. She wanted me
to hand over to her, for safe keeping in her corsage,
those same reels which Dædalus had entrusted to me,
claiming that to wind and unwind such things was a
woman's job (one, in fact, in which she was particularly expert) and that she wanted to spare me the
bother of attending to it. But in reality she hoped in
this way to remain the mistress of my fate, a thing to
which I would not consent at any price. Moreover, I
had another suspicion: Ariadne would be reluctant to
unwind, where every turn of the reel allowed me to
stray farther from herself; she might hold back the
thread, or pull it toward her; in such a case I should
be prevented from going in as far as I wanted. I
therefore stood my ground, in the face even of that
last argument of woman, a flood of tears—knowing
well that if one once begins to yield one's little finger,
they are quick to snap up the whole arm, and the rest
with it.

This thread was neither of linen nor of wool.
Dædalus had made it from some unknown material,
which even my sword, when I experimented with a
little piece, was powerless to cut. I left the sword in
Ariadne's care, being determined (after what Dædalus
had said to me about the superiority that man owes
wholly to his instruments, and the decisive role of

these in my victories over the monsters)—being determined, as I say, to subdue the Minotaur with the strength of my bare hands. When, after all this, we arrived before the entrance to the labyrinth, a portal embellished with that double ax which one saw everywhere in Crete, I entreated Ariadne on no account to stir from the spot. She insisted that she should herself tie the end of the thread to my wrist, with a knot that she was pleased to call a lover's; she then glued her lips to my own and held them there for what seemed to me an interminable time. I was longing to get on.

My thirteen companions, both male and female, had gone on ahead, Pirithoüs among them; I found them in the first big room, already quite fuddled by the vapors. I should have mentioned that, together with the thread, Dædalus had given me a piece of rag drenched with a powerful specific against the gases, and had pressed me most particularly to employ it as a gag. (This also Ariadne had taken in hand, as we stood before the entrance to the labyrinth.) Thanks to it, and though hardly able to breathe, I was able in the midst of these intoxicating vapors to keep my head clear and my will taut. I was rather suffocated, all the same, because, as I've said before, I never feel really well when I'm not in the open air, and the artificial atmosphere of that place was oppressive to me.

Unreeling the thread, I penetrated into a second room, darker than the first; then into another, still darker; then into a fourth, where I could only grope my way. My hand, brushing along the wall, fell upon the handle of a door. I opened it, and stepped into brilliant sunshine. I was in a garden. Facing me, and stretched at length upon a flowery bed of buttercups,

pansies, jonquils, tulips, and carnations, lay the
Minotaur. As luck would have it, he was asleep. I
ought to have hurried forward and taken advantage
of this, but something held me back, arrested my arm:
the monster was beautiful. As happens with centaurs
also, there was in his person a harmonious blending
of man and beast. On top of this, he was young, and
his youthfulness gave an indefinable bloom to his good
looks; and I am more vulnerable to such things than
to any show of strength. When faced with them, I
needed to call upon all my reserves of energy. For one
never fights better than with the doubled strength of
hatred; and I could not hate the Minotaur. I even
stood still for some time and just looked at him. But
he opened one eye. I saw then that he was completely witless, and that it was time for me to set
about my task. . . .

What I did next, what happened, I cannot exactly
recall. Tightly as I had been gagged, my mind had
doubtless been benumbed by the gases in the first
room; they affected my memory, and if in spite of this
I vanquished the Minotaur, my recollection of the
victory is confused, though on the whole somewhat
voluptuous. That must be my last word, since I refuse
to invent. I have also many dreamlike memories of
the charms of that garden; it so went to my head that
I thought I could never bear to leave it; and it was
only reluctantly that, after settling with the Minotaur,
I rewound my thread and went back to the first room,
there to rejoin my companions.

They were seated at table. Before them a massive
repast had been spread (how or by whom I cannot
say). They were busy gourmandizing, drinking heav-
ily, making passes of love at one another, and braying

like so many madmen or idiots. When I made as if to take them away, they replied that they were getting on very well and had no thought of leaving. I insisted, saying that I had come to deliver them. "Deliver us from what?" they shouted; and suddenly they all banded together and covered me with insults. I was very much distressed, because of Pirithoüs. He hardly recognized me, forswore virtue, made mock of his own good qualities, and told me roundly that not for all the glory in the world would he consent to give up his present enjoyments. All the same, I couldn't blame him for it, because I knew too well that, but for Dædalus' precautions, I should have foundered in the same way, and joined in the chorus with him and with the others. It was only by beating them up, it was only by punching them and kicking them hard on their behinds, that I got them to follow me; of course there was also the fact that they were so clogged by drink as to be incapable of resistance.

Once out of the labyrinth, how slowly and painfully they came back to their senses and reassumed their normal selves! This they did with great sadness. It appeared to them (so they told me afterwards) as if they were climbing down from some high peak of happiness into a dark and narrow valley. Each rebuilt for himself the prison in which every man is his own jailor and from which he could never again escape. Pirithoüs, however, soon showed himself aghast at his momentary degradation, and he promised to redeem himself, in his own eyes and in mine, by an excess of zeal. An occasion was offered to him, not long afterwards, to give me proof of his devotion.

TEN

I HID NOTHING from him; he knew my feelings for Ariadne, and their decline. I did not even hide from him that, child though she might still be, I was very much taken with Phædra. She used often at that time to play on a swing strung up between the trunks of two palm trees; and when I saw her at the top of her flight, with the wind lifting her short skirts, my heart would miss a beat. But when Ariadne appeared, I looked the other way and dissembled my feelings as best I could, for fear of arousing in her the jealousy of an elder sister. Still, thwarted desires are not healthy. But if I was to abduct her, and thus bring off the audacious project that was beginning to simmer in my heart, I should need to employ a ruse of some sort. Then it was that Pirithoüs was able to help me by devising a plan stamped with all his fertile ingenuity. Meanwhile our stay in the island was dragging on, though both Ariadne and myself were obsessed with the idea of getting away. But what Ariadne didn't know was that I was resolved not to leave without Phædra. Pirithoüs knew it, and this is how he helped me.

He had more freedom than I—Ariadne stuck to me like a ball-and-chain—and he passed his leisure in the study and observation of the customs of Crete. "I think," he said to me one morning, "that I've got just

what we want. You know that Minos and Rhadamanthus, those two model legislators, have drawn up
a code of morals for the island, paying particular
attention to pederasty. As you know, too, the Cretans
are especially prone to this, as is evident from their
culture. So much so, in fact, that every adolescent who
reaches manhood without having been chosen by
some older admirer becomes ashamed and regards his
neglect as dishonorable; for if he is good-looking,
people generally conclude that some vice of heart or
mind must be the cause. Young Glaucus, the son of
Minos, who is Phædra's absolute double, confided to
me his anxiety in this respect. His friendless state
causes him much distress. I made the vain suggestion
that no doubt his princely rank has discouraged
admirers; he replied that this, though possible, did not
make his position in any way less painful, and that
people ought to realize that it was also a grief to
Minos; and that Minos as a rule disregards all distinc-
tions of rank and position. All the same, he would
certainly be flattered if an eminent prince like yourself were to be kind enough to take an interest in his
son. It occurred to me that Ariadne, who shows herself so importunately jealous of her sister, would have
no such feelings about her brother. There is hardly a
single instance of a woman taking serious notice of the
love of a man for a boy; in any case, she would think
it unbecoming to show resentment. You need have no
fear on that score."

"What!" I shouted. "Can you think that fear would
ever stop me? But though I am a Greek, I do not feel
myself drawn in any way toward people of my own
sex, however young and attractive they may be. In

this I differ from Hercules, and would gladly let him keep his Hylas. Your Glaucus may be like my Phædra, but it is she whom I desire, not he."

"You haven't grasped what I mean," he resumed, "I'm not suggesting you should take Glaucus in her place, but simply that you should pretend to take him, in order to deceive Ariadne and let her believe, and everybody else, that Phædra, whom you are carrying off, is Glaucus. Now listen and follow me carefully. One of the customs of the island, and one that Minos himself instituted, is that the lover assumes complete charge of the child whom he covets, and takes him to live with him, under his roof, for two months; after which period the child must announce publicly whether or not his lover has given him satisfaction and treated him properly. To take the supposed Glaucus under your roof, you must put him aboard the ship that brought us here from Greece. Once we are all assembled, with the crypto-Phædra safe in our hands, we must up-anchor; Ariadne will have to be there, since she assumes that she will be going with you; then we shall put out with all speed to the open sea. The Cretans have a large fleet, but their ships are not so fast as ours, and if they give chase we can easily outdistance them. Tell Minos about this project. You may be sure that he'll smile on it, provided you let him believe that Glaucus, and not Phædra, is involved; for, as for Glaucus, he could hardly hope to secure a better master and lover than yourself. But tell me: is Phædra willing?"

"I don't know as yet. Ariadne takes good care never to leave me alone with her, so that I've had no chance to sound her. . . . But I don't doubt that she will be ready to follow me, when she realizes that I prefer her to her sister."

It was Ariadne who had to be approached first. I took her into my confidence, but deceitfully of course, and according to our agreed procedure.

"What a wonderful plan!" she cried. "And how I shall enjoy traveling with my small brother! You've no idea how charming he can be. I get on very well with him and in spite of the difference in our ages I am still his favorite playmate. Nothing could be better for broadening his mind than to visit a foreign country. At Athens he can perfect his Greek, which he already speaks passably, though with a bad accent; that will soon be put right. You will set him the best of examples, and I only hope he will grow to be like you."

I let her talk. The wretched girl could not foresee what fate was in store for her.

Glaucus had also to be warned, lest any hitch should occur. Pirithoüs took charge of this, and told me later that the boy was at first bitterly disappointed. Only after an appeal to his better sentiments did he decide to join in the game; or rather, I should say, to drop out of it and yield up his place to his sister. Phædra had also to be informed. She might have started screaming if we had tried to abduct her by force or surprise. But Pirithoüs exploited with great skill the malicious pleasure that both children would not fail to take in gulling their elders—Glaucus his parents, and Phædra her sister.

Phædra duly rigged herself out in Glaucus' everyday clothes. The two were of exactly the same build, and when she had bound up her hair and muffled the lower part of her face, it was impossible for Ariadne not to mistake her identity.

It was certainly disagreeable for me to have to deceive Minos, who had lavished upon me every mark of his confidence, and had told me of the good influence that he expected me, as an older person, to have upon his son. And I was his guest, too. Of course I was abusing my position. But it was not, and indeed it is never, a part of my character to allow myself to be stopped by scruples. The voices of gratitude and decency were shouted down by the voice of desire. The end justifies the means. What must be must be.

Ariadne was first on board, in her anxiety to secure comfortable quarters. As soon as Phædra arrived, we could make off. Her abduction took place not at nightfall, as had at first been agreed, but after the family dinner, at which she had insisted on appearing. She pleaded that as she had formed the habit of going to her room immediately after dinner, her absence could not, she thought, be remarked before the morning of the next day. So everything went off without a hitch, and I was able to disembark with Phædra, a few days later, in Attica, having meanwhile dropped off her sister, the beautiful and tedious Ariadne, at Naxos.

I learned on arriving at our territory that when Ægeus, my father, had seen in the distance the black sails (those sails which I had omitted to change), he had hurled himself into the sea. I have already touched on this in a few words; I dislike returning to it. I shall add, however, that I had dreamed, that last night of our voyage, that I was already king of Attica. Be that as it may, or as it might have been, this was, for the whole population and for myself, a day of rejoicing for our happy return and my promotion to the throne, and a day of mourning for the death of my father. I therefore gave orders that in the rites for the day lamentations should alternate with songs of joy; and in these songs and dances we took a prominent part—my companions, now so implausibly restored to their homes, and myself. Joy and desolation: it was fitting that the people should be made to explore, at one and the same time, these two extremes of feeling.

ELEVEN

PEOPLE SOMETIMES reproached me afterwards for my conduct toward Ariadne. They said I had behaved like a coward; that I should not have abandoned her, or at any rate not on an island. Possibly; but I wanted to put the sea between us. She was after me, hunting me down, marking me for the kill. When she got wind of my ruse and detected her sister beneath her brother's clothes, she set up the devil's own noise, broke into a series of rhythmical screams, upbraided me for my treachery; and when, in my exasperation, I told her that I did not intend to take her farther than the first island at which the wind, now suddenly risen, would allow or compel us to make landfall, she threatened me with a long poem she proposed to write on the subject of this infamous desertion. I told her at once that she could not do better; the poem promised to be very good, as far as I could judge from her frenzied and lyrical tones; moreover, it would serve as a distraction, and she would undoubtedly soon find in it the best solace for her grief. But all this only vexed her the more. Such are women, when one tries to make them see reason. For my part, I always allow myself to be guided by an instinct in which, by reason of its greater simplicity, I have perfect confidence.

The island in question was Naxos. One story has it that, some time after we had abandoned her, Dionysus went there to join her, and indeed married her; all of which may be a way of saying that she found consolation in drink. People say that on their wedding day the god made her a present of a crown, the work of Hephæstus, which now forms one of the constellations; and that Zeus welcomed her on Olympus and made her immortal. She was even mistaken, they say, for Aphrodite. I let people talk, and myself, in order to cut short hostile rumors, did my best to confirm her divine rank by founding a cult in her honor. I also went out of my way to be the first to dance my reverences there. May I be allowed to remark that, but for my desertion, she would have enjoyed none of these great advantages?

Certain imaginary incidents have enriched the mythology of my person: the abduction of Helen, the descent into hell with Pirithoüs, the rape of Proserpine. I took care never to deny these rumors, for they all enhanced my prestige. I even improved upon some of them, in order to confirm the people in beliefs that they are all too inclined, in Attica, to discard. Popular emancipation is a good thing; irreverence quite another.

The truth is that after my return to Athens I remained faithful to Phædra. I took both the woman and the city for my bride. I was a husband, and the son of a dead king: I was a king. My days of adventure are over, I used to repeat to myself; where I had sought to conquer, I now sought to rule.

This was not easy. Athens at that time really did not exist. In Attica a mass of petty townships disputed for predominance; whence continual brawling, besieging, and strife. The essential thing was to secure a strong central unit of government—a thing I obtained only with great difficulty. I brought both strength and cunning to the task.

Ægeus, my father, thought he could assure his own authority by perpetuating these quarrels. Considering, myself, that the well-being of the citizens is compromised by such discords, I traced the source of most of the evils to the general inequality of wealth and the desire to increase one's own fortune. Myself caring little for the acquisition of wealth, and preoccupied with the public good as much as, if not more than, with my own, I set an example of plain living. By an equal division of all properties, I abolished at one blow both the fact of supremacy and the rivalries it had provoked. This was a drastic measure, which no doubt pleased the poor (the great majority, that is to say) but antagonized the rich, whom I had thereby dispossessed. These, though few in number, were clever men. I summoned the most important among them, and said:

"Personal merit is the only thing to which I attach any importance; I recognize no other scale of values. You have made yourselves rich by ingenuity, practical knowledge, and perseverance; but also, and more often, by injustice and abuse. Your private rivalries are compromising the security of a state that I intend to be a great power, beyond the reach of your intrigues. Only thus will it be able to resist foreign invasion, and prosper. The accursed love of money that torments you does not bring you happiness, for one can truly call it insatiable. The more people have, the more they want. I shall therefore curtail your fortunes; and by force (I possess it) if you do not submit peaceably to the curtailment. For myself I shall keep only the preservation of the laws and the

command of the army. I care very little for the rest.
I mean to live, now that I am king, just as simply as
I have lived hitherto, and in the same style as the
humblest of my subjects. I shall see that the laws are
respected, and that I myself am respected, if not
feared. I mean to have it said among our neighbors
that Attica is ruled, not by a tyrant, but by a government of the people; for each citizen of the state shall
have an equal right to sit on the council, irrespective
of his birth. If you do not side willingly with all this,
I shall find ways, as I said, to compel you.

"I shall raze and destroy utterly your little courts
of local justice and your regional council chambers,
and I shall assemble, beneath the Acropolis, the capital city which already bears the name of Athens. And
it is this name of Athens that for the races of the
future—and this I promise to the gods who show me
favor—will be a name of wonders. I dedicate my city
to Pallas. Now go, all of you, and take my words as
meant."

Then, suiting my example to my words, I stripped
myself of all royal authority, stepped back into the
ranks, and was not afraid to show myself to the public
without escort, like a simple citizen; but I gave my
attention unceasingly to public affairs, maintaining
peace and watching over the good order of the state.

Pirithoüs, after hearing me address the men of
wealth, said to me that he thought my speech sublime,
but ridiculous. Because, he argued: "Equality is not
natural among men; I would go farther and say that
it is not desirable. It is a good thing that the superior
men should rise above the vulgar mass to the full
height of their eminence. Without emulation, rivalry,
and jealousy, that mob will be forever a formless,

stagnant, wallowing mass. There must be some leaven to make it rise; take care that it doesn't rise against yourself. Whether you like it or not, and though you may succeed in your wish and achieve an initial leveling by which each man starts on the same plane and with an equal chance, yet differences of talent will soon bring about differences of station; in other words, a downtrodden people and an aristocracy."

"Good gods!" That set me off again. "I certainly expect that, and I hope it won't be long in coming. But in the first place I don't see why the people should be downtrodden if the new aristocracy, to which I shall give all the support in my power, is, as I would have it, an aristocracy not of wealth, but of intellect."

And then, in order to increase the power and importance of Athens, I made it known that there would be an impartial welcome for everyone, no matter whence he came, who might choose to come and settle there. And criers were sent throughout the neighboring countries to carry this message: "Peoples all, make haste to Athens!"

The news spread far and wide. And was it not through this that Œdipus, the fallen monarch, saddest and noblest of derelicts, made his way from Thebes to Attica, there to seek help and protection, there to die? Because of which I was able later to secure for Athens the blessing that the gods had conferred on his ashes. Of this I shall have more to say.

I promised to all newcomers indifferently the same rights as were enjoyed by those who were natives of Athens or who had settled there earlier; any necessary discrimination could await the proofs of experience. For good tools reveal their quality only after use, and

I wished to judge nobody except according to his services.

So that if I was later obliged none the less to admit differences among the Athenians (and consequently to admit a hierarchy), I allowed this only in order to ensure that the state would in general function better. Thus it is that, thanks to me, the Athenians came to deserve, among all the other Greeks, the fine name of "people," which was commonly bestowed upon them and upon them only. There lies my fame, far surpassing that of my earlier feats; a fame to which neither Hercules attained, nor Jason, nor Bellerophon, nor Perseus.

Pirithoüs, alas! the companion of my youthful exuberances, later fell away from me. All those heroes whom I have named, and others too, like Meleager and Peleus, never prolonged their career beyond their first feats, or sometimes beyond a single one. For myself, I was not content with that. "There is a time for conquest," I used to say to Pirithoüs, "a time for cleansing the earth of its monsters, and then a time for husbandry and the harvesting of well-cherished land; a time to set men free from fear, and then a time in which to find employment for their liberty, in which to profit by the moment of ease and coax it into bloom." And that could not be achieved without discipline: I would not admit that, as with the Bœotians, man should make himself his own boundary, or aim merely at a mediocre happiness. I thought that man was not and would never be free, and that it would not be a good thing if he were. But I couldn't urge him forward without his consent; nor could I obtain that consent without leaving him (leaving the people, at any rate) the illusion of liberty. I wanted to edu-

cate him. I would not allow him to become in any
degree content with his lot, or to resign himself to
furrow his brow in perpetuity. Humanity (such was
always the cast of my thought) can do more and
deserves better. I remembered the teaching of Dædalus, who wanted to enrich mankind with all the spoils
of the gods. My great strength was that I believed in
progress.

So Pirithoüs and I parted company. In my youth he
had been my constant companion, and often an invaluable aide. But I realized that constancy in friendship can prevent a man from advancing—can even
pull him backwards; after a certain point one can only
go forward alone. As Pirithoüs was a man of sense, I
still listened to what he said, but that was all. He himself was growing old, and whereas he had once been
enterprise itself, he now allowed wisdom to degenerate into temperance. His advice was now always for
restriction and restraint.

"Mankind isn't worth all this trouble," he would say.
And I would reply: "Well, what else is there to think
about, except mankind? Man has not yet said his last
word."

"Don't get excited," he used to reply. "Haven't you
done enough? Now that the prosperity of Athens is
assured, it is time for you to rest on your laurels and
savor the happiness of married life."

He urged me to pay more attention to Phædra and
there for once he was right. For I must now tell of
how the peace of my fireside was disturbed, and what
a hideous price was expected by the gods in return
for my successes and my self-conceit.

TWELVE

I HAD UNLIMITED CONFIDENCE in Phædra. I had watched her grow more beautiful month by month. She was the very breath of virtue. I had withdrawn her at so early an age from the pernicious influence of her family that I never conceived she might carry within her a full dose of inherited poison. She obviously took after her mother, and when she later tried to excuse herself by saying that she was not responsible, or that she was foredoomed, I had to own that there was something in it. But that was not all: I also believe that she had too great a disdain for Aphrodite. The gods avenge themselves, and it was in vain that Phædra later strove to appease the goddess with an added abundance of offerings and supplications. For Phædra was pious, in spite of everything. In my wife's family everyone was pious. But it was no doubt regrettable that not everyone addressed his devotions to the same god. With Pasiphaë, it was Zeus; with Ariadne, Dionysus. For my own part, I reverenced above all Pallas Athene, and next Poseidon, to whom I was bound by a secret tie, and who, unfortunately for me, had similarly bound himself always to answer my prayers, so that I should never beseech him in vain. My son whose mother had been the Amazon, and whom I set above all the others, devoted himself to Artemis the huntress. He was as chaste as she—as chaste as I, at his age, had been dissolute. He used to run naked through moonlit woods and thickets; detested the court, formal parties, and, above all, the society of women, and was only happy when, with his bearhounds, he could go hunting for wild beasts and follow them to the topmost mountain or the last recesses of a valley. Often, too, he broke in wild horses, tamed them on the seashore, or rode them at a full gallop into the sea. How I loved him then! Proud, handsome, unruly; not to me, whom he held in veneration, nor to the laws: but he despised the conventions that prevent a man from asserting himself and wear out his merits in futility. He it was whom I wanted for my heir. I could have slept quietly, once the reins of state were in his unsullied hands; for I knew that he would be as inaccessible to threats as to flatteries.

That Phædra might fall in love with him I realized only too late. I should have foreseen it, for he was very like me. (I mean, like what I had been at his age.) But I was already growing old, and Phædra was still astonishingly young. She may still have loved me, but it was as a young girl loves her father. It is not good, as I have learned to my cost, that there should be such a difference of age between husband and wife. Yet what I could not forgive her was not her passion (natural enough, after all, though half-incestuous), but that, when she realized she could not satisfy her desire, she should have accused my Hippolytus and imputed to him the impure longings that were consuming her. I was a blind father, and a too trustful husband; I believed her. For once in my life I took a woman at her word! I called down the vengeance of the gods upon my innocent son. And my prayer was heard. Men do not realize, when they address themselves to the gods, that if their prayers are answered, it is most often for their misfortune. By a sudden, passionate, mindless impulse I had killed my son. And I am still inconsolable. That Phædra, awakened to her guilt, should at once afterwards have wrought justice upon herself, well and good. But now that I cannot count even upon the friendship of Pirithoüs, I feel lonely; and I am old.

Œdipus, when I welcomed him at Colonus, had been driven from Thebes, his fatherland; without eyes, dishonored, and wretched as he was, he at least had his two daughters with him, and in their constant tenderness he found relief from his sufferings. He had failed in every part of what he had undertaken. I have succeeded. Even the enduring blessing that his ashes are to confer upon the country where they are laid—even this will rest, not upon his ungrateful Thebes, but upon Athens.

I am surprised that so little should have been said about this meeting of our destinies at Colonus, this moment at the crossroads when our two careers confronted each other. I take it to have been the summit and the crown of my glory. Till then I had forced all life to do obeisance to me, and had seen all my fellow men bow in their turn (excepting only Dædalus, but he was my senior by many years; besides, even Dædalus gave me best in the end). In Œdipus alone did I recognize a nobility equal to my own. His misfortunes could only enhance his grandeur in my eyes. No doubt I had triumphed everywhere and always; but on a level which, in comparison with Œdipus, seemed to me merely human—inferior, I might say. He had held his own with the Sphinx; had stood man upright before the riddle of life and dared to oppose him to the gods. How then, and why, had he accepted defeat? By putting out his eyes, had he not even contributed to it? There was something, in this dreadful act of violence against himself, that I could not contrive to understand. I told him of my bewilderment. But his explanation, I must admit, hardly satisfied me —or else I did not fully understand it.

"True," he said, "I yielded to an impulse of rage— one that could only be directed against myself; against whom else could I have turned? In face of the immeasurable horror of the accusations I had just discovered, I felt an overwhelming desire to make a protest. And besides, what I wanted to destroy was not so much my eyes themselves as the canvas they held before me; the scenery before which I was struggling, the falsehood in which I no longer believed; and this so as to break through to reality.

"And yet, no! I was not really thinking of anything very clearly; I acted rather by instinct. I put out my eyes to punish them for having failed to see the evidence that had, as people say, been staring me in the face. But, to speak the truth—ah, how can I put it to you? . . . Nobody understood me when I suddenly cried out: 'O darkness, my light!' And you also, you don't understand it—I feel that distinctly. People heard it as a cry of grief; it was a statement of fact. It meant that in my darkness I had found a source of supernatural light, illuminating the world of the spirit. I meant: 'Darkness, thou art henceforth my light.' And at the moment when the blue of the sky went black before me, my inward firmament became bright with stars."

He was silent and for some moments remained deep in meditation. Then he went on:

"As a young man, I passed for one who could see the future. I believed it myself, too. Was I not the first, the only man, to solve the riddle of the Sphinx? Only since my eyes of flesh were torn with my own hand from the world of appearances have I begun, it seems to me, to see truly. Yes; at the moment when the outer world was hidden forever from the eyes of my body, a kind of new eyesight opened out within myself upon the infinite perspectives of an inner world, which the world of appearances (the only one which had existed for me until that time) had led me to disdain. And this imperceptible world (inaccessible, I mean, to our senses) is, I now know, the only true one. All the rest is an illusion, a deception, moreover, that disturbs our contemplation of what is divine. Tiresias, the blind sage, once said to me: 'Who wishes to see God must first cease to see the world'; and I didn't understand him then: just as you, yourself, O Theseus, do not understand me now."

"I shall not attempt to deny," I replied, "the importance of this world beyond temporal things of which your blindness has made you aware; but what I still cannot understand is why you oppose it to the outer world in which we live and act."

"Because," said Œdipus, "for the first time, when with my inward eye I perceived what was formerly hidden from me, I suddenly became aware of this fact: that I had based my earthly sovereignty upon a crime, and that everything which followed from this was in consequence tainted; not merely all my personal decisions, but even those of the two sons to whom I had abandoned my crown—for I at once stepped down from the slippery eminence to which my crime had raised me. You must know already to

what new villainies my sons have allowed themselves
to stoop, and what an ignominious doom hangs over
all that our sinful humanity may engender; of this my
unhappy sons are no more than a signal example. For,
as the fruits of an incestuous union, they are no doubt
doubly branded; but I believe that an original stain of
some sort afflicts the whole human race, in such a
way that even the best bear its stripe, and are vowed
to evil and perdition; from all this man can never
break free without divine aid of some sort, for that
alone can wash away his original sin and grant him
amnesty."

He was silent again for a few moments, as if pre-
paring to plunge still deeper, and then went on:

"You are astonished that I should have put out my
eyes. I am astonished myself. But in this gesture, in-
considered and cruel as it was, there may yet be
something else: an indefinable secret longing to follow
my fortunes to their farthest limit, to give the final
turn of the screw to my anguish, and to bring to a
close the destiny of a hero. Perhaps I dimly foresaw
the grandeur of suffering and its power to redeem;
that is why the true hero is ashamed to turn away
from it. I think that it is in fact the crowning proof
of his greatness, and that he is never worthier than
when he falls a victim; then does he exact the gratitude of heaven, and disarm the vengeance of the gods.
Be that as it may, and however deplorable my mis-
takes may have been, the state of unearthly beatitude
that I have been able to reach is an ample reward for
all the ills that I have had to suffer—but for them,
indeed, I should doubtless never have achieved it."

"Dear Œdipus," I said, when it was plain that he
had finished speaking, "I can only congratulate you

on the kind of superhuman wisdom you profess. But my thoughts can never march with yours along that road. I remain a child of this world, and I believe that man, be he what he may, and with whatever blemishes you judge him to be stained, is in duty bound to play out his hand to the end. No doubt you have learned to make good use even of your misfortunes, and through them have drawn nearer to what you call the divine world. I can well believe, too, that a sort of benediction now attaches to your person, and that it will presently be laid, as the oracles have said, upon the land in which you will take your everlasting rest."

I did not add that what mattered to me was that this blessing should be laid upon Attica, and I congratulated myself that the god had made Thebes abut upon my country.

If I compare my lot with that of Œdipus, I am content: I have fulfilled my destiny. Behind me I leave the city of Athens. It has been dearer to me even than my wife and my son. My city stands. After I am gone, my thoughts will live on there forever. Lonely and consenting, I draw near to death. I have enjoyed the good things of the earth, and I am happy to think that after me, and thanks to me, men will recognize themselves as being happier, better, and more free. I have worked always for the good of those who are to come. I have lived.

THE TEXT *of this book was set on the Linotype in Caledonia, a face that belongs to the family of printing types called "modern face" by printers—a term used to mark the change in style of type-letters that occurred about 1800. Caledonia borders on the general design of Scotch Modern, but is more freely drawn than that letter.*

VINTAGE FICTION, POETRY, AND PLAYS

V-814   **ABE, KOBO** / The Woman in the Dunes
V-2014   **AUDEN, W. H.** / Collected Longer Poems
V-2015   **AUDEN, W. H.** / Collected Shorter Poems 1927-1957
V-102   **AUDEN, W. H.** / Selected Poetry of W. H. Auden
V-601   **AUDEN, W. H. AND PAUL B. TAYLOR (trans.)** / The Elder Edda
V-20   **BABIN, MARIA-THERESA AND STAN STEINER (eds.)** / Borinquen: An Anthology of Puerto-Rican Literature
V-271   **BEDIER, JOSEPH** / Tristan and Iseult
V-523   **BELLAMY, JOE DAVID (ed.)** / Superfiction or The American Story Transformed: An Anthology
V-72   **BERNIKOW, LOUISE (ed.)** / The World Split Open: Four Centuries of Women Poets in England and America 1552-1950
V-321   **BOLT, ROBERT** / A Man for All Seasons
V-21   **BOWEN, ELIZABETH** / The Death of the Heart
V-294   **BRADBURY, RAY** / The Vintage Bradbury
V-670   **BRECHT, BERTOLT (ed. by Ralph Manheim and John Willett)** / Collected Plays, Vol. 1
V-759   **BRECHT, BERTOLT (ed. by Ralph Manheim and John Willett)** / Collected Plays, Vol. 5
V-216   **BRECHT, BERTOLT (ed. by Ralph Manheim and John Willett)** / Collected Plays, Vol. 7
V-819   **BRECHT, BERTOLT (ed. by Ralph Manheim and John Willett)** / Collected Plays, Vol. 9
V-841   **BYNNER, WITTER AND KIANG KANG-HU (eds.)** / The Jade Mountain: A Chinese Anthology
V-207   **CAMUS, ALBERT** / Caligula & Three Other Plays
V-281   **CAMUS, ALBERT** / Exile and the Kingdom
V-223   **CAMUS, ALBERT** / The Fall
V-865   **CAMUS, ALBERT** / A Happy Death: A Novel
V-626   **CAMUS, ALBERT** / Lyrical and Critical Essays
V-75   **CAMUS, ALBERT** / The Myth of Sisyphus and Other Essays
V-258   **CAMUS, ALBERT** / The Plague
V-245   **CAMUS, ALBERT** / The Possessed
V-30   **CAMUS, ALBERT** / The Rebel
V-2   **CAMUS, ALBERT** / The Stranger
V-28   **CATHER, WILLA** / Five Stories
V-705   **CATHER, WILLA** / A Lost Lady
V-200   **CATHER, WILLA** / My Mortal Enemy
V-179   **CATHER, WILLA** / Obscure Destinies
V-252   **CATHER, WILLA** / One of Ours
V-913   **CATHER, WILLA** / The Professor's House
V-434   **CATHER, WILLA** / Sapphira and the Slave Girl
V-680   **CATHER, WILLA** / Shadows on the Rock
V-684   **CATHER, WILLA** / Youth and the Bright Medusa
V-140   **CERF, BENNETT (ed.)** / Famous Ghost Stories
V-203   **CERF, BENNETT (ed.)** / Four Contemporary American Plays
V-127   **CERF, BENNETT (ed.)** / Great Modern Short Stories
V-326   **CERF, CHRISTOPHER (ed.)** / The Vintage Anthology of Science Fantasy

V-293 **CHAUCER, GEOFFREY** / The Canterbury Tales (a prose version in Modern English)
V-142 **CHAUCER, GEOFFREY** / Troilus and Cressida
V-723 **CHERNYSHEVSKY, N. G.** / What Is to Be Done?
V-173 **CONFUCIUS (trans. by Arthur Waley)** / Analects
V-155 **CONRAD, JOSEPH** / Three Great Tales: The Nigger of the Narcissus, Heart of Darkness, Youth
V-10 **CRANE, STEPHEN** / Stories and Tales
V-126 **DANTE, ALIGHIERI** / The Divine Comedy
V-177 **DINESEN, ISAK** / Anecdotes of Destiny
V-431 **DINESEN, ISAK** / Ehrengard
V-752 **DINESEN, ISAK** / Last Tales
V-740 **DINESEN, ISAK** / Out of Africa
V-807 **DINESEN, ISAK** / Seven Gothic Tales
V-62 **DINESEN, ISAK** / Shadows on the Grass
V-205 **DINESEN, ISAK** / Winter's Tales
V-721 **DOSTOYEVSKY, FYODOR** / Crime and Punishment
V-722 **DOSTOYEVSKY, FYODOR** / The Brothers Karamazov
V-780 **FAULKNER, WILLIAM** / Absalom, Absalom!
V-254 **FAULKNER, WILLIAM** / As I Lay Dying
V-884 **FAULKNER, WILLIAM** / Go Down, Moses
V-139 **FAULKNER, WILLIAM** / The Hamlet
V-792 **FAULKNER, WILLIAM** / Intruder in the Dust
V-189 **FAULKNER, WILLIAM** / Light in August
V-282 **FAULKNER, WILLIAM** / The Mansion
V-339 **FAULKNER, WILLIAM** / The Reivers
V-412 **FAULKNER, WILLIAM** / Requiem For A Nun
V-381 **FAULKNER, WILLIAM** / Sanctuary
V-5 **FAULKNER, WILLIAM** / The Sound and the Fury
V-184 **FAULKNER, WILLIAM** / The Town
V-351 **FAULKNER, WILLIAM** / The Unvanquished
V-262 **FAULKNER, WILLIAM** / The Wild Palms
V-149 **FAULKNER, WILLIAM** / Three Famous Short Novels: Spotted Horses, Old Man, The Bear
V-45 **FORD, FORD MADOX** / The Good Soldier
V-7 **FORSTER, E. M.** Howards End
V-40 **FORSTER, E. M.** / The Longest Journey
V-187 **FORSTER, E. M.** / A Room With a View
V-61 **FORSTER, E. M.** / Where Angels Fear to Tread
V-219 **FRISCH, MAX** / I'm Not Stiller
V-842 **GIDE, ANDRE** / The Counterfeiters
V-8 **GIDE, ANDRE** / The Immoralist
V-96 **GIDE, ANDRE** / Lafcadio's Adventures
V-27 **GIDE, ANDRE** / Strait Is the Gate
V-66 **GIDE, ANDRE** / Two Legends: Oedipus and Theseus
V-958 **von GOETHE, JOHANN WOLFGANG (ELIZABETH MAYER, LOUISE BOGAN & W. H. AUDEN, trans.)** / The Sorrows of Young Werther and Novella
V-300 **GRASS, GUNTER** / The Tin Drum
V-425 **GRAVES, ROBERT** / Claudius the God
V-182 **GRAVES, ROBERT** / I, Claudius
V-717 **GUERNEY, B. G. (ed.)** / An Anthology of Russian Literature in the Soviet Period: From Gorki to Pasternak

V-829   **HAMMETT, DASHIELL** / The Big Knockover
V-2013   **HAMMETT, DASHIELL** / The Continental Op
V-827   **HAMMETT, DASHIELL** / The Dain Curse
V-773   **HAMMETT, DASHIELL** / The Glass Key
V-772   **HAMMETT, DASHIELL** / The Maltese Falcon
V-828   **HAMMETT, DASHIELL** / The Red Harvest
V-774   **HAMMETT, DASHIELL** / The Thin Man
V-781   **HAMSUN, KNUT** / Growth of the Soil
V-896   **HATCH, JAMES AND VICTORIA SULLIVAN (eds.)** / Plays by and About Women
V-15   **HAWTHORNE, NATHANIEL** / Short Stories
V-610   **HSU, KAI-YU** / The Chinese Literary Scene: A Writer's Visit to the People's Republic
V-910   **HUGHES, LANGSTON** / Selected Poems of Langston Hughes
V-304   **HUGHES, LANGSTON** / The Ways of White Folks
V-158   **ISHERWOOD, CHRISTOPHER AND W. H. AUDEN** / Two Plays: The Dog Beneath the Skin and The Ascent of F6
V-295   **JEFFERS, ROBINSON** / Selected Poems
V-380   **JOYCE, JAMES** / Ulysses
V-991   **KAFKA, FRANZ** / The Castle
V-484   **KAFKA, FRANZ** / The Trial
V-841   **KANG-HU, KIANG AND WITTER BYNNER** / The Jade Mountain: A Chinese Anthology
V-508   **KOCH, KENNETH** / The Art of Love
V-915   **KOCH, KENNETH** / A Change of Hearts
V-467   **KOCH, KENNETH** / The Red Robbins
V-82   **KOCH, KENNETH** / Wishes, Lies and Dreams
V-134   **LAGERKVIST, PAR** / Barabbas
V-240   **LAGERKVIST, PAR** / The Sibyl
V-776   **LAING, R. D.** / Knots
V-23   **LAWRENCE, D. H.** / The Plumed Serpent
V-71   **LAWRENCE, D. H.** / St. Mawr & The Man Who Died
V-329   **LINDBERGH, ANNE MORROW** / Gift from the Sea
V-822   **LINDBERGH, ANNE MORROW** / The Unicorn and Other Poems
V-479   **MALRAUX, ANDRE** / Man's Fate
V-180   **MANN, THOMAS** / Buddenbrooks
V-3   **MANN, THOMAS** / Death in Venice and Seven Other Stories
V-297   **MANN, THOMAS** / Doctor Faustus
V-497   **MANN, THOMAS** / The Magic Mountain
V-86   **MANN, THOMAS** / The Transposed Heads
V-36   **MANSFIELD, KATHERINE** / Stories
V-137   **MAUGHAM, W. SOMERSET** / Of Human Bondage
V-720   **MIRSKY, D. S.** / A History of Russian Literature: From Its Beginnings to 1900
V-883   **MISHIMA, YUKIO** / Five Modern Nō Plays
V-151   **MOFFAT, MARY JANE AND CHARLOTTE PAINTER** / Revelations: Diaries of Women
V-851   **MORGAN, ROBIN** / Monster
V-926   **MUSTARD, HELEN (trans.)** / Heinrich Heine: Selected Works
V-901   **NEMIROFF, ROBERT (ed.)** / Les Blancs: The Collected Last Plays of Lorraine Hansberry
V-925   **NGUYEN, DU** / The Tale of Kieu

V-125   **OATES, WHITNEY J. AND EUGENE O'NEILL, Jr. (eds.)** / Seven Famous Greek Plays

V-973   **O'HARA, FRANK** / Selected Poems of Frank O'Hara

V-855   **O'NEILL, EUGENE** / Anna Christie, The Emperor Jones, The Hairy Ape

V-18   **O'NEILL, EUGENE** / The Iceman Cometh

V-236   **O'NEILL, EUGENE** / A Moon For the Misbegotten

V-856   **O'NEILL, EUGENE** / Seven Plays of the Sea

V-276   **O'NEILL, EUGENE** / Six Short Plays

V-165   **O'NEILL, EUGENE** / Three Plays: Desire Under the Elms, Strange Interlude, Mourning Becomes Electra

V-125   **O'NEILL, EUGENE, JR. AND WHITNEY J. OATES (eds.)** / Seven Famous Greek Plays

V-151   **PAINTER, CHARLOTTE AND MARY JANE MOFFAT** / Revelations: Diaries of Women

V-907   **PERELMAN, S. J.** / Crazy Like a Fox

V-466   **PLATH, SYLVIA** / The Colossus and Other Poems

V-232   **PRITCHETT, V. S.** / Midnight Oil

V-598   **PROUST, MARCEL** / The Captive

V-597   **PROUST, MARCEL** / Cities of the Plain

V-596   **PROUST, MARCEL** / The Guermantes Way

V-600   **PROUST, MARCEL** / The Past Recaptured

V-594   **PROUST, MARCEL** / Swann's Way

V-599   **PROUST, MARCEL** / The Sweet Cheat Gone

V-595   **PROUST, MARCEL** / Within A Budding Grove

V-714   **PUSHKIN, ALEXANDER** / The Captain's Daughter and Other Stories

V-976   **QUASHA, GEORGE AND JEROME ROTHENBERG (eds.)** / America a Prophecy: A Reading of American Poetry from Pre-Columbian Times to the Present

V-80   **REDDY, T. J.** / Less Than a Score, But A Point: Poems by T. J. Reddy

V-504   **RENAULT, MARY** / The Bull From the Sea

V-653   **RENAULT, MARY** / The Last of the Wine

V-24   **RHYS, JEAN** / After Leaving Mr. Mackenzie

V-42   **RHYS, JEAN** / Good Morning Midnight

V-319   **RHYS, JEAN** / Quartet

V-2016   **ROSEN, KENNETH (ed.)** / The Man to Send Rain Clouds: Contemporary Stories by American Indians

V-976   **ROTHENBERG, JEROME AND GEORGE QUASHA (eds.)** / America a Prophecy: A New Reading of American Poetry From Pre-Columbian Times to the Present

V-41   **SARGENT, PAMELA (ed.)** / Women of Wonder: Science Fiction Stories by Women About Women

V-838   **SARTRE, JEAN-PAUL** / The Age of Reason

V-238   **SARTRE, JEAN-PAUL** / The Condemned of Altona

V-65   **SARTRE, JEAN-PAUL** / The Devil & The Good Lord & Two Other Plays

V-16   **SARTRE, JEAN-PAUL** / No Exit and Three Other Plays

V-839   **SARTRE, JEAN-PAUL** / The Reprieve

V-74   **SARTRE, JEAN-PAUL** / The Trojan Women: Euripides

V-840   **SARTRE, JEAN-PAUL** / Troubled Sleep

V-607   **SCORTIA, THOMAS N. AND GEORGE ZEBROWSKI (eds.)** / Human-Machines: An Anthology of Stories About Cyborgs

V-330   **SHOLOKHOV, MIKHAIL** / And Quiet Flows the Don

V-331   **SHOLOKHOV, MIKHAIL** / The Don Flows Home to the Sea

V-447   **SILVERBERG, ROBERT** / Born With the Dead: Three Novellas About the Spirit of Man

V-945   **SNOW, LOIS WHEELER** / China On Stage

V-133   **STEIN, GERTRUDE** / Autobiography of Alice B. Toklas

V-826   **STEIN, GERTRUDE** / Everybody's Autobiography

V-941   **STEIN, GERTRUDE** / The Geographical History of America

V-797   **STEIN, GERTRUDE** / Ida

V-695   **STEIN, GERTRUDE** / Last Operas and Plays

V-477   **STEIN, GERTRUDE** / Lectures in America

V-153   **STEIN, GERTRUDE** / Three Lives

V-710   **STEIN, GERTRUDE & CARL VAN VECHTEN (ed.)** / Selected Writings of Gertrude Stein

V-20   **STEINER, STAN AND MARIA-THERESA BABIN (eds.)** / Borinquen: An Anthology of Puerto-Rican Literature

V-770   **STEINER, STAN AND LUIS VALDEZ (eds.)** / Aztlan: An Anthology of Mexican-American Literature

V-769   **STEINER, STAN AND SHIRLEY HILL WITT (eds.)** / The Way: An Anthology of American Indian Literature

V-768   **STEVENS, HOLLY (ed.)** / The Palm at the End of the Mind: Selected Poems & A Play by Wallace Stevens

V-278   **STEVENS, WALLACE** / The Necessary Angel

V-896   **SULLIVAN, VICTORIA AND JAMES HATCH (eds.)** / Plays By and About Women

V-63   **SVEVO, ITALO** / Confessions of Zeno

V-178   **SYNGE, J. M.** / Complete Plays

V-601   **TAYLOR, PAUL B. AND W. H. AUDEN (trans.)** / The Elder Edda

V-443   **TROUPE, QUINCY AND RAINER SCHULTE (eds.)** / Giant Talk: An Anthology of Third World Writings

V-770   **VALDEZ, LUIS AND STAN STEINER (eds.)** / Aztlan: An Anthology of Mexican-American Literature

V-710   **VAN VECHTEN, CARL (ed.) AND GERTRUDE STEIN** / Selected Writings of Gertrude Stein

V-870   **WIESEL, ELIE** / Souls on Fire

V-769   **WITT, SHIRLEY HILL AND STAN STEINER (eds.)** / The Way: An Anthology of American Indian Literature

V-2028   **WODEHOUSE, P. G.** / The Code of the Woosters

V-2026   **WODEHOUSE, P. G.** / Leave It to Psmith

V-2027   **WODEHOUSE, P. G.** / Mulliner Nights

V-607   **ZEBROWSKI, GEORGE AND THOMAS N. SCORTIA (eds.)** / Human-Machines: An Anthology of Stories About Cyborgs